Job at the Top

THE CHIEF EXECUTIVE
IN LOCAL GOVERNMENT

Sir John Boynton

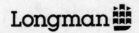

Longman Group Limited
Longman House, Burnt Mill, Harlow, Essex, CM20 2JE, UK

© Longman Group Limited 1986

First published 1986

British Library Cataloguing in Publication Data
  Boynton, Sir John, 1918–
Job at the top: the chief executive in local government.
1. Local officials and employees — England
I. Title
352'.008'0942   J53173

ISBN 0–582–90113–8

Printed and bound in Great Britain by
Biddles Ltd, Guildford and King's Lynn

Contents

Preface

Those who pick up this book expecting to find a treatise about the science of management or theories on the structure of organizations will look in vain.

This is a personal and practical view based upon my experience as chief executive of one of the largest local authorities in England, with my vision sharpened by five years post retirement work, mainly in the private sector. Those five years have seen many changes, with a great increase in central government control, and a range of problems arising from the assertive political stance of some local councils. Never has it been more necessary for chief executives in local government to have a clear understanding of their role.

The chief executive's job comprises many elements to be found in other senior posts in the public service – and indeed also in the private sector, for there is a common dimension to management wherever it is practised. I hope therefore that this book may interest a wider audience than just those in local government. And not only those at the top, but those who aspire to get there.

With women holding chief executive posts and so many local councils emphasising that they are equal opportunity employers, I ought to say that I have used the masculine gender as embracing the feminine throughout the text, so that for example 'he' and 'his' might equally be 'she' and 'hers'.

I am grateful to Professor John Stewart of the Institute of Local Government Studies at Birmingham University who read the first draft, and suggested that I should add some personal recollections. I hope that these, interspersed between the pages, will help to illuminate the text.

June 1985   John Boynton

Acknowledgements: The publishers wish to thank HMSO for permission to reproduce copyright material on pages 11, 12, 38, 39, 40, 41, 72, 73, and 74; the Chief Executives' Joint Negotiating Committee pages 6–10, and Cheshire County Council pages 67–71.

1 The job

To describe the chief executive in British local government it seems necessary to fall back upon the old story of the small boy asked to describe an elephant which he had seen for the first time on a visit to the zoo. He could not, the small boy said, describe it; but he would know one if he saw one again.

Councils who have a genuine chief executive, know they have one. Departmental heads know they have one. The staff know they have one. Ministries know they have one.

The genuine chief executive is indeed easily recognizable. There are several hundred people who hold the office of chief executive in Britain today. Not all these are genuinely chief executives. They hold the title but the role they perform lacks some essential part.

Some councils have a chief executive who is a good coordinator who prevents interdepartmental absurdities. Coordination is necessary but it is not the whole job.

Some councils have a chief executive who is good at oiling the wheels. He dispels friction between councillors: between councillors and staff and between the authority and the trade unions. Oiling the wheels is necessary but it is not the whole job.

Some councils have a chief executive who looks and plays the part, and handles the public relations of the council with skill. Good internal and external relations are necessary but are not the whole job.

Some councils have a chief executive who is politically adroit, and provides a sensitive interface between the elected leadership and the administration. Political know-how is necessary but it is not the whole job.

The whole job is something more than all these. It is to provide leadership to the paid staff. It is to provide it at all times, when the going is rough and people do not want to be led, as well as when they do.

The chief executive understands that leadership should not infringe the rights of elected members to decide policy. Yet he will not shrink from taking action because some might label the issue as political. He will not kick difficult balls over the political touch line.

The chief executive understands also that he has to provide effective management of the work and business of the council. Yet he will not be overawed by concepts of scientific management, recognizing that management primarily involves the development and training of people.

The chief executive must assume a responsibility for the whole of the affairs and activities of the authority. His corporate role must spring from a conviction that the authority is – or can be – something more than the sum of its different parts.

The received wisdom

The received wisdom about the job of the chief executive is contained in Appendix 1.1. This sets out the duties and responsibilities of the chief executive as promulgated by the National Joint Negotiating Committee for chief executives in England and Wales. There is a notable omission in this nationally agreed job definition from that recommended by the Bains Committee in their report *The New Local Authorities; Management and Structure* produced in 1972 for the Associations of Local Authorities. The Committee's recommended job description set out in Appendix 1.2 said that the chief executive should 'have authority over all other officers so far as that is necessary for the efficient management and execution of the council's functions'. At national level the employers shrank from conceding the supremacy of the chief executive, though individual councils were left a discretion to do so if they desired – and several have.

Appendix 1.3 contains a summary of the role of the chief executive prepared by D. R. Kaye of Arthur Andersen, the internationally known firm of accountants and management consultants.

These lists of duties or tasks are helpful in giving some idea of the different roles which a chief executive may be expected to play. But they provide no more than chapter headings, with little in the way of elaboration or explanation. What for example is meant by 'personally control the process for handling corporate matters' in Mr Kaye's paper? Without some indication of the meaning of 'corporate matters', it is not clear what processes might require personal control by the chief executive. The range of local authority services is very wide, with little obvious connection between one service and another. Roads have little to do with education or housing with markets, or markets with leisure. All are 'services' in the sense that they serve the public: and in some, the various facets of the operation touch the facets of others in an obvious way. For example, there are well-known areas of interaction between education, libraries and leisure services; between social services and housing, and between town planning and highways.

However, for the most part the head of a department sees himself as providing a self-contained, free-standing and discrete service. He will recognize well-established points of contact with other departments: but for the rest sees himself as running a separate business. Indeed if there is to be professional competence and pride in performance, the departmental chief officer's perception of his own role must not be needlessly interfered with. If some part of his activities is to be labelled 'corporate' and as a result its handling is to be personally controlled by the chief executive, the departmental head needs to understand the rationale behind the decision.

Clearly the corporate role of the chief executive is an important one. He has to have a responsibility for the whole of the affairs and activities of the local authority. He is the top professional, the head of the paid service. Yet with defined responsibilities, he has under the British system little defined power. He does not hire and fire. He does not appoint or dismiss the chief officers or other staff. Indeed as we have seen his authority over them may be ambiguous. He is not usually responsible for preparing and presenting the budget. Nor does he usually have power to approve departmental expenditure. By contrast the city manager in many American cities would have all these powers. A few chief officer appointments would require the council's consent, but the city manager's responsibility for the paid staff would be backed by his power of appointment and dismissal. His position as manager would be further recognized by a duty to present the budget to the council. It is all clear and simple to understand in such a system.

In Britain we have introduced a concept and a title, chief executive, which cannot be simply described because the system defines responsibilities, but does not back them with defined powers. In Britain there has been a preoccupation in the post-war years with the areas and functions of local authorities. Reorganization of the basic concepts of administration has been neglected. These concepts are still those of the turn of the century. Power resides in the councillors collectively. They have the ability since 1974 to delegate responsibility to officers but this is generally done for marginal decisions and not for central core functions.

The chief executive, whilst not vested with powers which would make his position and role easily explainable, has nevertheless potentially enormous influence. This may derive from his own personal input into the whole range of the council's activities. He is in a unique position to make his presence felt. But it derives even more from his ability to have access to the leadership at elected level. The chief executive should be in the confidence of that leadership. He should enjoy their confidence: if he loses it, he will be ineffectual. His power-base will have been eroded.

Any discussion of the job of the chief executive must address itself to the fundamental question of the relationships with councillors and the political leadership.

Job security

If the chief executive's role is not backed by clear cut authority, his power-base is made more tenuous by the absence of any job security. A few councils have made appointments of chief executives and chief officers on fixed term contracts. But for the most part appointments are terminable on notice, and the main redress against unfair action lies in the procedural code of the Joint Negotiating Committee forming part of Appendix 1 to this chapter. Prior to the reorganization of 1974 clerks of county councils could only be appointed and dismissed with the consent of the Secretary of State. Town and district council clerks held a statutory office which had to be filled – the office (and with it the office-holder) could not vanish overnight in the course of some organizational review. All these safeguards disappeared in 1974 in the interests of giving local authorities greater freedom. It is ironic that this should have occurred at a time when party politics were greatly to increase in local government and when, in many areas a new type of councillor was to emerge, suspicious of officers and sometimes resentful of advice. Whilst a fixed term contract offers a degree of security, it may be thought also to encourage nonrenewal, particularly where renewal occurs under a different political regime to that existing when the appointment was made.

Few would deny that a problem exists and that the task of giving impartial and independent advice was never more difficult (even dangerous) – or more necessary. The chief executive's exposed position at the top makes him the most vulnerable of all the senior staff. It is a job which requires sensitivity, integrity resolve and patience. It is not a job for the faint hearted. It is a job which chief executives are carrying out with courage and skill in most local authorities in Britain today. When one considers the tenuous and ill defined power-base from which the chief executive in Britain has to operate it is astonishing that so many do so well.

THE REJECTED EXECUTIVE

In the aftermath of reorganization, several chief executives fell foul of their new authorities, and as the then chairman of the Chief Executives' Association I was involved in assisting them.

One of the common elements in each of these cases was that the chief executive had been taken by surprise by the action of the political leaders. There had been no warning, no hint of impending disaster. For their part, councillors were adamant that no rapprochement was possible. Confidence in the chief executive was said to have been eroded and to be incapable of restoration.

In the pre-reorganization days, it was possible outside the larger urban areas for a clerk of a council or a town clerk (to use the pre-1974 titles) to stay fairly aloof from councillors, meeting them on formal occasions, largely in committee meetings. There was usually a need to develop a relationship with the person or persons where power resided, for example Lord Macclesfield in Oxfordshire, but the job could be done in many authorities without studying the needs of the council and councillors as a whole. I recall accompanying a deputation to Dr Hugh Dalton in 1950 and as we and the councillors left the Ministry in Whitehall, the then clerk of the council grabbed my arm and said 'Hurry along or we might have to lunch with them'. This little incident reflected an attitude not uncommon in councils at the time, but now a rarity.

Today's chief executive cannot adopt the stance in relation to the council 'You do your job and leave me to do mine'. One of those whose interests I defended, remarked to me in bewilderment that his new chairman (who had just asked the chief executive to take early retirement) 'had only asked to see me on two or three occasions since he took over'. You could not say that a rift had developed between them, for they had never been together. The onus for building a bridge to the councillors individually, collectively and in their party groupings must surely rest with the chief executive. Councillors may occasionally indicate what is expected or required of the paid administration. More often they look to the chief executive's training and experience to provide answers to questions which the elected representatives perceive only dimly.

In my experience, councillors (even tough and capable ones) are unwilling to oversee the performances of their chief executive. They are unlikely to give timely warning and counsel when things may be taking a wrong course, but will let things run on till eventually some drastic action is suggested. (The position in industry and commerce seems to be much the same) The man at the top has to be master of his own destiny. He must be ready to pay the ultimate price for failure in performance – removal from the scene by one means or *another. He is unlikely to get any warning that such a threat hangs over him.*

Appendix 1.1

Extracts from the conditions of service of chief executives in England and Wales, promulgated by the Joint Negotiating Committee.

Definition of chief executive

30 The term 'chief executive' means the officer who is the head of the council's paid service. The duties and responsibilities of the post shall be settled by the individual employing authority, but might well for example include the following:-

(i) Responsibility as leader of the officers' management team for

    a securing co-ordination of advice on the forward planning of objectives and services and for leading the management team in securing a corporate approach to the affairs of the authority generally; and

    b the efficient and effective implementation of the council's programmes and policies and for ensuring that the resources of the authority are most effectively deployed towards those ends.

(ii) Advising the council and its committees on all matters upon which his advice is necessary and the right of attendance at all committees of the council and all sub-committees and working parties.

(iii) Advising or make suitable arrangements for advising the mayor or chairman of the council on all matters within the duties of that office.

Whole-time service

31 He shall devote his whole-time service to the work of the council and shall not engage in any other business or take up any other additional appointment without the express consent of the council. He shall not subordinate his duty as chief executive to his private interests or put himself in a position where his duty and private interest conflict.

Fidelity bond

32 He shall enter into such fidelity bond as the council may require, the council paying the premiums thereof.

Advice to political groups

33 He shall not be required to advise any political group of the council, either as to the work of the group or as to the work of the council, neither shall he be required to attend any meetings of any political group. This shall be without prejudice to any arrangements to the contrary which may be made in agreement with the chief executive and which includes adequate safeguards to preserve the political neutrality of the chief executive in relation to the affairs of the council.

Conduct of negotiations

34 No major negotiations relating to the functions or duties of the council shall be initiated or carried on by any other officer of the council except with the cognisance of the chief executive.

35 Reserved

PROCEDURES RELATING TO REDUNDANCY, INCAPABILITY AND DISCIPLINE

Application

42 Procedures are set out below for use in cases relating to redundancy, incapability and discipline. The Joint Secretaries of the JNC should be notified as soon as it is proposed to use any of these procedures and both parties are also recommended to contact the appropriate Side Secretary as early as possible to ascertain whether more detailed assistance might be desirable.

Conciliation

43 The Joint Secretaries are available at any stage in the procedures to act in an impartial conciliation role if required to do so by either party (although conciliation is more likely to be of assistance before matters have progressed too far).

Termination of employment on the grounds of redundancy

44 If, following a proper investigation, a proposal to abolish the post of Chief Executive has been put forward by an employing authority, or an appropriate committee or sub-committee of an employing authority, so that there is a possibility of the redundancy of the post holder, then a period of consultation is necessary in accordance with Section 99 of the Employment Protection Act 1975. The information required to be provided under Section 99 should be communicated in writing to:-

(i) The Chief Executive and a representative of an independent Trade Union recognised by the employers for collective bargaining purposes for the Chief Executive; and

(ii) The Joint Secretaries of the Joint Negotiating Committee.

Receipt of this information by the Chief Executive should commence the consultation period which shall be of at least 28 days (four weeks) duration. During the course of these consultations the possibility of alternative employment should be considered. In the light of these consultations the employing authority should first consider the proposals and any representations made by or on behalf of the Chief Executive and only then take whatever decision it considers appropriate. The employing authority should bear in mind throughout this procedure the desirability of treating the matter as confidential until a final decision has been reached.

Incapability

Note The procedure may need adaptation where medical fitness is in question.

45 Where there is a question of the capability of a Chief Executive to carry out his duties and responsibilities to the satisfaction of the employing authority it should normally be for a group of not less than three elected members appointed by the Chairman or Leader of the Council as appropriate to carry out a preliminary and careful examination of the matter. The appointed elected members should consider any relevant evidence in this connection, and also bear in mind the degree of confidence of elected members in the Chief Executive. As part of this consideration the elected members should provide the opportunity to the Chief Executive and to any trade union which he nominates as representing him or to some other person of his choice to offer comments and should take those into account. Matters may be settled satisfactorily as a result of this discussion, whether on the lines suggested in paragraph 46 or otherwise. However if the elected members concerned are satisfied that the matter requires further consideration the procedures set out in paragraphs 47–51 below shall be applied as appropriate to facilitate further examination, according to the circumstances of the individual case.

46 If as a result of either the initial consideration by the appointed elected members or a full examination by a committee or sub-committee of members it is concluded that the Chief Executive is not carrying out his duties and responsibilities to the level of capability that the employing authority genuinely believes is required, it should be considered whether an alteration in duties and responsibilities may be appropriate. If this is not regarded as appropriate, members should consider the possibility of either a recorded oral warning or a written warning with the provision of a reasonable amount of time for the Chief Executive to meet the requirements of his post or (if there has been a previous written warning or if after full examination by a Committee or sub-committee of members the incapability is judged to be fundamental and irremediable) dismissal with notice. A satisfactory outcome may alternatively be achieved by the Chief Executive undertaking actively to seek other employment, resigning or accepting retirement.

Discipline

Note Authorities are recommended to have full regard to the principles and standards set out in the ACAS Code of Practice on Disciplinary Procedures.

The provisions in relation to Gross Misconduct are set out in Paragraph 53.

47 Where a question of discipline is raised in connection with the Chief Executive it should normally be for a group of not less than three elected members appointed by the Chairman or Leader of the Council as appropriate to carry out a preliminary and careful investigation. As part of this investigation the elected members concerned should take into account any explanations given by the Chief Executive. During the investigation the Chief Executive has the right to be represented by his trade union or some other person of his choice. If, following this preliminary investigation, the elected members are satisfied that the matter requires further consideration, either the appropriate committee or sub-committee if there is one, or otherwise a specially constituted committee or sub-committee, should fully investigate the matter.

If at any stage it is felt appropriate, the Chief Executive may (subject to whatever consultation or approval may be required under the authority's standing orders) be suspended from duty on full pay pending further investigation. Written notice stating the reason for any such suspension shall be given.

48 The decision to have a full investigation should be communicated in writing to:-

(i) the Chief Executive and at his request to any Trade Union of which he is a member and

(ii) the Joint Secretaries of the Joint Negotiating Committee.

The Chief Executive should be given not less than 10 working days' notice of the meeting of the appropriate committee or sub-committee, and should at the same time be given full details of the complaints made against him. Within this time the Chief Executive has the right to request:-

(i) further details of the complaints made, and

(ii) a postponement of the meeting for a period to be agreed between the parties or, in default of agreement, for a period not exceeding 14 days.

The Chief Executive shall be informed of his rights to challenge the case against him and to present his case to the appropriate committee or sub-committee; to be represented at the meeting by his Trade Union representative or some other person of his choice; and to call any witnesses whom he considers appropriate and produce any documents which he considers relevant.

49 At the hearing, after any statement and evidence (including witnesses) in support of the complaint, the Chief Executive may himself give evidence, call witnesses and produce documents. A person making any statement on behalf of the employing authority, the Chief Executive (or his representative) and each witness may be questioned on his statement or evidence by the other party and by members of the Committee. The person presenting the complaint and finally the Chief Executive or his representative should have the right to sum up at the end of the hearing, and in no case should the Committee hear the party without the other being present.

50 The investigating committee or sub-committee shall recommend a course of action to the full council or other committee with the power of final decision, and the Chief Executive should be informed of their recommendations at the earliest opportunity, or in any case at least 10 working days before the meeting of the council (or committee). The Chief Executive shall have the opportunity to appeal against the recommendation by presenting a written submission when the matter is considered by the council or appropriate committee. He or his representative shall have the right to attend this meeting and speak to the written submission. Members who sat on the investigatory committee may attend, and clarify points of information as necessary, but should not participate during the final consideration in the meeting of the council or appropriate committee.

51 The council or appropriate committee should consider the recommendation in the light of the written and oral submissions made, and reach a final decision. The employing authority should bear in mind throughout all stages of the procedure the desirability of treating the matter as confidential until a final decision has been reached.

52 As a result of either initial investigation by the appointed elected members or full investigation by a committee or sub-committee of members, the action taken could, according to the severity of the case, take any of the following forms:-

> Recorded oral warning
> Written warning
> Suspension on half or no pay for a specified period
> Relegation (i.e. reduction in salary) for a specified period
> An invitation to resign or accept retirement
> Dismissal with notice, etc.
> (see footnote after paragraph 53)

Gross misconduct

53 When a case appears to be one of gross misconduct then normally the Chief Executive should (subject to whatever consultation or approval may be required under the authority's standing orders) be suspended from duty on full pay pending further investigation. The disciplinary procedures set out in paragraphs 47–52 will not normally be appropriate. An investigation should be conducted by elected members as speedily as possible and as part of this investigation the Chief Executive must be given the opportunity to submit his explanations (if he so wishes). For Gross Misconduct a Chief Executive can be dismissed without notice.

Note In the case of dismissal the employing authority should bear in mind the provisions of Sections 53 and 57 of the Employment Protection (Consolidation) Act 1978 relating to the provision of written statements of the reasons for dismissal and general provisions relating to fairness of dismissal respectively.

Appendix 1.2

Extract from the report of the committee on *The New Local Authorities; Management and Structure* published by Her Majesty's Stationery Office, 1972.

JOB SPECIFICATION FOR A CHIEF EXECUTIVE

1 The Chief Executive is the head of the Council's paid service and shall haveuthority over all other officers so far as this is necessary for the efficient management and execution of the council's functions.

2 He is the leader of the officers' management team and through the Policy and Resources Committee, the Council's principal adviser on matters of general policy. As such it is his responsibility to secure co-ordination of advice on the forward planning of objectives and services and to lead the management team in securing a corporate approach to the affairs of the authority generally.

3 Through his leadership of the officers' management team he is responsible for the efficient and effective implementation of the Council's programmes and policies and for securing that the resources of the authority are most effectively deployed towards those ends.

4 Similarly he shall keep under review the organisation and administration of the authority and shall make recommendations to the Council through the Policy and Resources Committee if he considers that major changes are required in the interests of effective management.

5 As head of the paid service it is his responsibility to ensure that effective and equitable manpower policies are developed and implemented throughout all departments of the authority in the interests both of the authority and the staff.

6 He is responsible for the maintenance of good internal and external relations.

Appendix 1.3

THE CHIEF EXECUTIVE ROLE

As we interpret it, the role of the chief executive should require him to:

personally control the process for handling corporate matters;

actively manage the relationship between members and officers;

coordinate the way business is handled at officer level, ensuring that individual responsibilities are well defined and timetables established;

intervene to resolve communications and other interdepartmental problems;

ensure that officers understand the views of members;

establish and encourage a high standard of work by officers, particularly in reporting to members and the management team;

counsel officers who have difficulty in achieving acceptable standards;

keep under review the organisation and administration of the authority and recommend any major changes required in the interests both of the authority and staff;

ensure that effective and equitable manpower policies are developed and implemented;

be responsible for maintaining good internal and external relations.

D. R. Kaye
Arthur Andersen

2 The professional team

The chief executive may be the leader of the professional team, but he needs to remember that it is a team and that the team is as important as the leader. The chief executive is not a one-man band. Even in the smaller local authorities, he heads up a large organization. Many of his problems will stem from the size of the staff complement. Knowing what is going on; communicating to and involving staff; motivation; securing a corporate approach – all these and many other aspects of management grow in difficulty as the size of the organization increases. The chief executive can only succeed if he can get his chief officers working with him. They in their turn need to secure the commitment of their own departments to the attitudes, policies and objectives which they have collectively agreed to.

Management by consent

Many would argue that the only successful management is management by consent. To get results by fear, by autocracy or by rewards and punishments may be necessary in particular organizations at particular times – and then usually with success only if employed for a limited period. In normal times, the chief executive should be seeking for the consent of his management team. Consent does not mean that everyone must agree whole-heartedly with every decision on every issue. Inevitably there will be times when someone goes along with a decision, willing to play his part, albeit with mental reservations. If the team leader ordinarily manages by consent, he will occasionally be allowed to impose his own view and his own solution on a reluctant team. If he has a good track record, and has been more often right in his judgement than wrong, he can sometimes lead the team into territory which left to themselves, the team would not venture into. This is what leadership is all about.

MANAGEMENT BY CONSENT

When I arrived in 1964 in Cheshire, I had one thing in my attache case – a sheet of A4 notepaper designed by Derek Birdsall, and geared to window envelopes. All this was somewhat revolutionary 20 years ago. The design was put before a surprised chief officers' meeting who agreed nevertheless to adopt it, for general use. Years later I discovered that one chief officer had a small stock printed for use only when writing to me. For the rest of the world he continued to use his fine Victorian letter heading, until he retired.
If you don't win their hearts and minds, you don't win.

Consideration of the chief executive's tenuous and ill-defined position, described in Chapter 1, reinforces the view that his task is to lead rather than to drive, to persuade rather than to coerce. He should not be deflected by opposition from pursuing courses he believes to be right. He should not fail to bring pressure to bear when it is needed. But his broad management stance should be to get commitment to the policies and objectives he seeks to introduce. He should not shrink from securing the backing of the political leadership for those policies and objectives, if this is the only way to make progress. However, if he always uses the fact of member support as a weapon in the battle to secure the response he wants, he is likely to lose the respect of the team.

ADMINISTRATIVE POLICY

We are used to saying that the council must settle policy. However, this does not mean that there cannot be policies relating to administration which do not directly impinge on the rights of elected members to settle levels of service and expenditure. Some of the early policies or objectives which I had set myself, after I had had time to study the local scene in Cheshire, included the following mainly 'administrative' matters:-

1   To secure that more senior appointments were made from outside – I felt that some departments were dangerously inbred.

2   *Where there was a choice, to aim for fewer better paid posts rather that more posts at the old salary levels.*

3   *To raise the level of capital expenditure achieved. In 1964 this was no more that 65% or so of the expenditure planned and budgetted for by the council.*

4   *To improve the deplorable working conditions of the Local Taxation and Licensing Department.*

5   *To increase central control over policies for recruitment training and salaries. In 1964 personnel work was centred on one officer in my department.*

There is inevitably an overlap between 'administrative' policies or objectives and council policies. Some administrative objectives may be capable of realization without action by the council. Raising the level of achieved capital spending would be an example. More often, the pursuit of an administrative objective will require some council approval. For example, improved personnel work could not easily have been introduced if the council had not voted the staff to do it. New offices were found for the Local Taxation and Licensing Department, but the council had to approve the additional rental and removal costs involved.

Policy does not necessarily have to flow downwards from the elected members to the paid staff. It can flow from the grass roots upwards, with ideas being aired in discussion or prepared as working papers for the council's leadership to consider.

The executive's department

Some readers might have expected this chapter to begin with a dissertation on the size and membership of the management team and the relationship of the chief executive to other departments. Should he, for example, be responsible for general committee administration as was the former town or county clerk? Or should he be quite independent, and if so, what assistance should he have?

Important though these issues are, experience suggests that the single most important factor in successful working is the attitude and approach of the chief executive.

There are successful chief executives, who, for reasons of economy or otherwise, have assumed the responsibility for what is elsewhere carried out by a secretary or director of administration. Indeed there are some who combine the duties of chief executive and finance director. They may have problems in persuading others that they are genuinely independent, and do not favour their own department. But the problem is not insurmountable.

There are successful chief executives who work with minuscule staff assistance – perhaps a secretary and a personal assistant. They depend for their success on establishing good working relationships with the director of finance and the person who manages the business of the council, whether titled secretary, director of administration, clerk and solicitor, or the like. These two officers preeminently hold the key to knowledge without which the chief executive would be emasculated.

There are successful chief executives who look to a support unit for the knowledge and help they need. The unit might contain corporate planners, research and intelligence personnel, economists, a public relations officer and an industrial promotion section. The central personnel staff might also report direct to the chief executive, as might the data-processing directorate and organization and methods officers. The chief executive who works in this way needs to be on his guard against taking on too much personal responsibility, so that he has no time to see the wood for the trees. He must ensure that the directors of administration and finance do not feel their positions to be threatened by the activities of the staff of the chief executive. The problems again are not insoluble. Good results can be obtained by many different arrangements, including variants on the structures outlined above.

The management team

A similar diversity of approach can be seen in the structure of the management team itself and its methods of working.

In some cases a small group may meet frequently and regularly perhaps the directors of administration and finance, under the chairmanship of the chief executive.

In others, a larger group may meet less frequently but also on a programmed basis. In between there may be meetings of a smaller informal group, either on a regular or impromptu basis.

A chief executive, on assuming responsibility in an authority, will find some accepted pattern. If he wishes to enlarge the management team, he will have fewer problems than if he wishes to exlude some who have hitherto participated. Those excluded may seek to rock the boat, even if the matter is handled with sensitivity. If the chief executive bears in mind that all these question of structure and organization are secondary to his personal attitude, example and performance, he will not waste energies on making changes for doctrinaire reasons. There is no one ideal way of working. The problems currently facing the authority, the abilities of the various chief officers, and past tradition and experience are all factors which will tend to shape the pattern.

In deciding upon the size of team he will rely on, the chief executive should remember that the heads of the big battalions are not always his best allies. Their departments may be large enough to feel self-sufficient. The head of a small department may seem more clearly the advantage of a corporate approach to may problems. Size of command does not reflect scale of ability. There are many admirable chief officers of smaller departments whose support can be harnessed to objectives which the chief executive wishes to pursue.

THE SUPPORTIVE SMALL DEPARTMENT

I can recall many instances where objectives I sought to achieve were warmly supported by officers like the county librarian, the chief fire officer or the chief inspector of trading standards. Central recruitment of juniors at the end of the school year is an example. The scheme provided an opportunity for proper induction, and in the less hard pressed days of the 1960s and 1970s, allowed supernumeraries to be recruited to cover future wastage. (Looking back, it is hard to recall that it was not easy to recruit junior staff in the middle of the school year). The smaller departments could see that the new policy would greatly help them, whereas one or two of the very largest could have implemented a similar policy single-handed. Another example would be a measure of central control on internal promotions to more senior posts. Smaller departments could see that if the big departments could promote their own staff without any outside scrutiny, there was little chance of their able staff moving sideways within the authority. Early experiments in central purchasing again were supported by those without the purchasing power to do well for themselves. When the heads of these departments spoke up in favour of change, it influenced the thinking of the meeting. I do not mean to imply that large departments were hidebound, merely that their size generated a feeling of self-sufficiency.

However the chief executive structures the management team, he should have a larger meeting several times a year at which all key post-holders can attend.

At such meetings, much of the agenda will originate directly in the chief executive's office. Other chief officers will put forward matters for discussion and there will be reports with major policy implications which require consideration by every member of the team. The chief executive through chairing these meetings will get to know his senior staff. Their reactions to items and reports will tell the chief executive much about the attitude and stance of each of them. There are optimists and pessimists; the touchy and the equable; the eager and the cautious. There are those who grumble at interference from the centre and others who complain that there is a lack of coherent central policy. There are loyal supporters but also those whose inner conviction is that they could do the job better than the chief executive. The knowledge of the strengths and weaknesses of the individual members who make up the top echelon of command will help the chief executive to decide which members will need support and encouragment, which will need a restraining hand from time to time, and the degree of advice and assistance each may need in a crisis, for example an awkward industrial dispute affecting some part of the service.

Counselling

Besides the regular meetings just described, the chief executive should arrange to see individual departmental heads at rather lengthy intervals say once every year or eighteen months. The object is to have an unhurried meeting, with the emphasis on what is usually called counselling. At least half a day needs to be allotted, and the chief executive needs to prepare himself in advance with the matters which on his side merit discussion. The areas which could feature on the agenda for such a meeting (besides problem areas already identified) might include the following:-

1   Are relations with chairman and councillors causing any problems? Acute problems will probably have come to light already, but there may be difficulties which the meeting will uncover and help to solve, e.g. by acting as a prelude to a later meeting with elected members. The chief executive has a key role to play in ensuring that the relationship between councillors and staff is satisfactory.

2   Is the performance of any senior staff member causing concern? With his detached position, the chief executive can sometimes take on board the counselling of a senior staff member, more easily and more successfully than the head of the department – or they may choose to do it together or simply leave it for the chief officer to go it alone.

3   What are the chief officer's ideas for his own career development? He may have hopes of a place on a longish management course (or if beyond the age group may wish his deputy to be considered). He may look for the chief executive's support in assuming membership of some government working party. The meeting is the time to discuss the chief officer's personal hopes for the future: the chief executive may be able to help, if he knows what each member of the team has by way of hopes and expectations for the future.

4 Where does the chief officer see the main thrust of his department as lying over the next year or two? What tangible objectives has he set for himself or his department? It might for example be to reduce the response time over some part of the service much used by the public. It might be to introduce data-processing to some area of work now reliant on manual effort. It might be to effect a defined economy in staff by better organization of work. The chief executive should encourage the setting of targets of this sort, selective targets limited in number with real prospects of achievement.

5 Has the chief officer any personal targets for the year ahead? These will vary greatly from one individual to another. One chief officer may be conscious that he is spending too much time outside the office. Another may aim to visit more of the establishments under his control during the next twelve months. One may aim to complete some research project. Another may aim personally to draft some policy manual or pamphlet of guidance circulating within his department.

6 Do the comparative financial and other statistics produced by the Audit Commission, the Chartered Institute of Public Finance and Accountancy and the Associations of Local Authorities suggest that there are areas of policy or administration which require examination? It may well be better to raise issues of this sort outside the budgetary process. The response may be less defensive. Steps may be taken for an objective look in a more measured way than would be the case at budget formulation.

7 Is the chief officer satisfied with the services provided centrally? The print unit, the organization and methods sections, the personnel officer, the staff canteen and staff welfare facilities, internal audit – time must be found to allow for criticisms or suggestions relating to these and similar services. By the same token, the chief executive should not put himself above criticism or review. Now is the time for the chief executive to put himself forward as a target, for in this way he may learn more than he expected.

Discussions of the sort described take time and courage; courage, that is, to raise the issues which really need examination. Before any chief executive embarks on counselling sessions with his senior colleagues, the objectives need to be explained and the purpose clarified. It is not a fault finding exercise. It is intended to help both sides in the discussion to do better. If the chief executive is younger than most of his chief officers, he may have to adjust his own attitudes before taking on a series of interviews. Nothing is worse than a bland discussion which touches no difficult ground, sets no targets and is merely an exercise in aimiable but pointless politeness. Used positively and unflinchingly, periodical sessions between chief executive and chief officers can do much good. On the whole it is best that these discussions are on a one-to-one basis. However, either party should be free to have someone join in for part of the time. A chief officer might want a deputy to explain a particular problem area. The chief executive for his part might see the wisdom of having the treasurer join him for some items. Much turns on the personalities involved and the traditions of working in the authority. The discussion is intended to be personal and privileged. Inviting outsiders to join in is best regarded as the exception rather than the rule.

Personal targets

If the chief executive is to ask others to set personal targets for themselves, he must be prepared to do so himself. It may be to ensure that some long running conflict is resolved. Or that a development scheme is finally completed. Or that an overdue policy statement sees the light of day. Or to be more available by reserving periods in the diary for the purpose. There are many possibilities, the essential factor being that success should be measurable. Setting a target is not the same as making a bland statement of good intention.

The targets once settled should be put in front of the management team and the larger meeting of all chief officers for their information. If the chief executive puts his personal cards on the table in this way, he displays his confidence in his team. He does not ask them to do things which he does not bother to do himself. Above all the process puts an emphasis on performance.

PERSONAL TARGETS

In 1977 I put in front of the chief officers' board some personal objectives of which the key ones were:

1   To be at my desk four days a week and to assist in this objective, to resign from two bodies on which I served. (I felt I was getting trapped in outside work).

2   To get the employment board operational by a high level of personal input – up to 25% of my time in the year.

The employment board was a new venture designed (a) to assess the problems of existing industries and commercial firms and help them to stay in Cheshire and (b) help in promotion of new employment opportunities.

There are some initiatives which can only succeed if driven from the top: so many good ideas fail because the author did not nurse them to the point where they could be free standing. Some indeed only survive through one man's personal commitment.

Team changes

From time to time there will be a vacancy at chief officer level. The opportunity to strengthen the team must then be seized and the chief executive should set aside the necessary time to be fully involved in the selection process. However well led, well organized and well trained, the management team is no stronger than its individual members. If a vacancy can be filled by the appointment of an able successor, whether an existing deputy or someone from outside, the performance of the whole team can be rejuvenated.

A problem which occasionally has to be faced is the fact that one member of the management team no longer measures up to the job. The problem may be incapable of solution by counselling. It is easy to find reasons for doing nothing about under- or non-performers: everyone shrinks from having to face a colleague with a critical view of his or her performance. Yet the issue has to be faced. It has to be faced in the interests of the staff of the department who will be acutely conscious of the ineffectiveness of the man at the top. It has to be faced in the interests of the organization as a whole. The chief executive must face it in his own interest. If he is seen to flinch from an obvious challenge, if he is seen not to have the fibre and toughness which the occasion may demand, he will lose respect and credibility.

His first step must be to discuss the matter with the political leadership to get their support to the action proposed and, if early retirement is involved, their agreement on fair, perhaps generous, terms. Only if he gets this support, can the chief executive take resolute action. In putting the case to councillors it should be possible to show that any severance costs involved will be more than offset in the longer term by gains in efficiency.

THE HARD DECISION

I listened to Sir Kenneth Durham, head of Unilever, talk about the problems of managing one of the world's largest businesses. Speaking of the need to deal with under-performers, Sir Kenneth said 'I don't start the meeting with pleasantries. I go straight into it and tell the man or woman that they are to be moved or demoted or retired. It is not an easy thing to do, so my way is to get the unpleasant part over with at the outset'. My own experience would endorse this. It is far from easy to tell a colleague that the council wish to see him retire early: or to tell one of your staff that unless he does better, you will take further action under the disciplinary code. Bernard Darwin the famous golf correspondent of The Times once wrote of the runner-up of the Open Championship 'He may have missed that three foot putt: but he is at home a loving husband and a good family man'. It is not easy to separate out in the mind what a man does and what a man is. Some of the least competent people I know were charming companions and good family men. Unfortunately today no organization can afford to pay for incompetence.

3 Committee work

Blessed is he who has nothing to say and cannot be persuaded to say it.

If an outsider telephones the chief executive's office, it is long odds that he will be advised that the chief executive is in committee, will be back at one o'clock and has another committee in the afternoon expected to last till five o'clock when the municipal telephone exchange closes down.

This is natural enough, for most council work is done through the committee system. The number of committee meetings has tended to increase since the introduction of attendance allowances for councillors, so that the need to have a view about committee work is more rather than less important today.

Attendance at committees can become a way of life. It can be a pleasant life. The work is not arduous, though lack of heating or ventilation may produce an element of physical discomfort. There is the illusion that one is making a useful contribution to the working of the authority, whilst the need to read papers and attend meetings provides a good reason for deferring difficult decisions on current problems. The gossip with councillors before and after the meeting can enliven the rather repetitive nature of the day's proceedings. Small wonder that some chief executives become 'committee men' immersed in the details of committee work and attending many, many meetings. Some chief executives take a radically different view. Committee meetings take up a great deal of time and the decisions to be reached have often been taken beforehand in a party caucus. So the chief executive decides that he should stay away as often as possible, leaving others to attend and briefing them as to any points he wishes them to raise. As practised by some chief executives, non-attendance can also become a way of life. The chief executive is rarely seen or heard by councillors, but concentrates on doing other things – and there are plenty of important things to do. It is difficult to disagree with the view that the time spent in committee is relatively unproductive, and on arguments of pure efficiency, the radical policy of non-attendance can be justified.

There are nevertheless three good reasons why the chief executive should seek some involvment with committee work:

1 A chief executive can only get to know the views and attitudes of councillors, the mood of the council, by contact with councillors. Committee work provides the principal opportunity for the learning process in many councils.

2 So much of the work of councils is done through committees that the chief executive needs to see the system in action to be able to gauge its efficiency.

3 By taking some committees personally, he can provide other staff with a model, based on his greater experience, of the way in which an adviser to a committee can assist in the dispatch of business.

Each of these three reasons needs some amplification.

The mood of the council

When a chief executive gets into difficulties with his council, the trouble can often be traced back to a failure on the chief executive's part to perceive what the council expected of him. At some point, he will be found to have been insensitive to the mood of the leadership. A chief executive cannot distance himself from councillors: he of all people must know how their minds may work. In some authorities this knowledge may be available through regular contact with the political leadership. In others, the existence of a members' and chief officers' canteen may provide opportunities for informal contact and discussion. In many councils, however, the principal point of contact will be through attendance at committees; and in these cases the chief executive may have to accept more calls on his time for committee attendance than would ideally be the case. The problems posed by the proliferation of meetings is well worth discussing with the council's leadership. It is not difficult to show the time demands posed by committee attendance, and to get agreement as to those committees at which the chief executive's attendance is regarded as obligatory. The chief executive should also get acceptance of the proposition that where he attends other committees for specific items, those will be taken in such a way as to keep to a reasonable minimum the time spent waiting for the items to be reached. (It is not always wise to take such items first, before the committee has become 'warmed up' with some routine business.)

The chief executive must be seen by councillors. He must be seen to be there, to be accessible. By one means or another he must get to know his council. He must be able to detect changes of mood or opinion. He may otherwise find himself out of touch and isolated – and inevitably therefore ineffectual. The means by which he keeps his finger on the pulse may vary, because councils are not all alike. But in many cases it will be primarily through committee attendance that these objectives are achieved. This does not mean attendance at all or most committees, or attendance for the whole of every agenda, or the same degree of attendance through the whole of the life of a council – the first year may require more, for example. A balance has to be struck. The comfortable life of 'the good committee man' must be rejected in favour of a compromise which leaves adequate time for the other important parts the chief executive should seek to play.

OUT OF STEP

I never much liked the title 'clerk of the county council'. My children were tired of explaining to their classmates that I did not just keep a ledger at county hall. The title is I suppose an example of those many pieces of British understatement, the title concealing the fact that the holder of the post had enormous influence in the county. I use the word influence rather than power, because what I lacked in clear cut powers, I made up in the ability to influence decisions on many matters. At any rate, I decided that the post should have a more up to date title, and persuaded a committee that the post be redesignated 'director general' following precedents elsewhere at the time. When the matter came before the county council for approval of the recommendation, member after member spoke against it. The word general seemed to hint at some sort of military takeover, and the experience of councillors in the army, under sergeants let alone generals retold at some length, were uniformly unfavourable. It was all very good humoured, and I tried to remain genial of countenance as the proposal was so to speak laughed out of court. I did not enjoy it.

The truth was that I had got out of touch with the mood of the council. The signals had been flown, but I had misread or ignored them. It was a salutary experience.

Sampling efficiency

The way in which committee business is transacted is a crucial test of
the efficiency of a local authority. It is one of the principal interfaces
between councillors and the administration. The first judgment which
councillors can make about the efficiency of the administration will
be based upon the quality of preparation of the committee business.
Do papers get out in time? Are reports long and ambiguous? Is the
agenda overloaded? Do long items of business get sent out late as
supplementary items? The answers to these and other questions will
shape the councillor's view as to the efficiency of the administration.
The chief executive cannot afford to distance himself from these
issues, even if he is assisted by a secretary or director of
administration.

One of the simplest methods of keeping this matter under review is
to attend a random selection of meetings of committees. This forces
the chief executive at least to peruse the circulated agenda. He will
soon hear at the committee if papers have arrived late, and will get a
feel as to the extent to which the paper work has contributed to the
success or otherwise of the proceedings.

Attendance at committees in this way needs to be distinguished
from attending as the principal adviser, to 'take the committee' in
local government jargon. Attending to form a view about the
efficiency of the proceedings, is a form of 'activity sampling'. It can be
unannounced. The chief executive should not sit next to the
chairman. He is there to hear and observe rather than contribute. He
will leave when he has seen and heard enough, and he should avoid
participating if he can. Because the chief executive goes to observe,
he need not prepare for the committee in the way which would be
necessary if he were to take it. This, and the ability to stay for as long
as fits in with his other duties, minimises the burden on his time.
Regular 'activity sampling' of different committees will enable him to
see his chief officers in action. It will also allow him to see where
different committee clerks have different practices, where minuting
styles differ and the extent to which departmental reports are prepared on different bases. Uniformity is said to be dull, but for a
councillor attending several committees, it is perplexing if each is a
separate world operating according to its own esoteric rules. By
attending in effect as a councillor the chief executive may well be
able to suggest lines for improvement and see where training and
development effort is needed.

If a chief executive intends to operate in the way described, the
secretary or director of administration and committee clerks need to
know what the practice will be. It is also helpful on the first occasion
with a particular chairman to give an informal notice of the variety: 'I
may drop in to your committee next week to hear the debate on the

report on X, which I hear is to come up.' This will avoid confusion as to the reason for what would otherwise be an unexpected appearance – though it can cause much interest among the rank and file as to why he is there. One spin-off arising from this practice is that it permits the chief executive to be seen at committees, to be seen to be there and accessible, without the burden involved in taking the committee. This can and should be left to the regular committee adviser and committee clerk.

The learning process

There can be few people in local government who have not at some stage in their career admired the performance and expertize in committee of a mature senior officer. There is indeed much that can be learned in this way from those more experienced in committee work.

The experienced man does not hog the discussion. He may know more about the item than anyone in the room, but he does not have to tell them everything he knows.

The experienced man does not reject all ideas that come from the floor of the house. He may know they are likely to prove impracticable, but he can get credit for having an open mind by agreeing to take them on board.

The experienced man does not evade a question. He may not know the answer, but he will then promise to obtain it and circulate it to the committee.

The experiences man does not always have to be right. He may have every reason in a complex matter for having misdirected himself at some point, but if so he will admit it and put the record straight.

The experienced man does not have to answer everything off the cuff. He may think he knows, but he will prefer to give a considered opinion later on at the next meeting.

The experienced man does not delight in telling the committee that the action proposed is illegal or surchargeable. He may say with sorrow that it is, but he will at the same time tell them that he will take advice as to how the action proposed might nevertheless lawfully be achieved.

The experienced man does not argue with other officials in front of the committee. It may be that there is a substantial difference of opinion hitherto undisclosed; but if so, he will ask that the matter be deferred so that, if possible, agreed advice can be tendered.

The experienced man does not try to score points off councillors: they are all entitled to his respect.

The experienced man does not refuse to apologize or withdraw.

He knows that in the heat of presentation, argument and debate, it is possible to go too far; but he will seek the committee's indulgence if quiet reflection makes him feel that he has done so.

The experienced man does not read his papers for the first time in the committee. He leaves that to councillors.

The experienced man earns his reputation when at the end of a long and apparently inconclusive debate, he reads out something which synthesizes the discussion and magically transforms it into a proposition which everyone is prepared to vote for in the un-challengeable belief that it is what they personally intended all along.

The chief executive should be an experienced man. He should go to some committees and speak on some items so that others can learn from his experience.

CHANGING TIMES

The clerk of a county council was bemoaning to me the election to his council of a large number of new and talkative councillors. 'In the old days' he lamented 'a new member had first to serve for three years on the Lunacy and Mental Deficiency Committee or the Smallholdings and Allotments Committee. He was not expected to open his mouth at county council meetings for the first twelve months. Now they expect places on major committees and talk at their first meeting.' Cheshire County Council in the 1960s sometimes displayed attitudes which had elsewhere largely disappeared. I recall once arriving five or ten minutes late for the Salaries and Estab-lishment Committee and Sir Wesley Emberton announced to laughter that the business had just been concluded. Cheshire Com-mittees in those days indeed rubber-stamped the recommendations of officials, just as in some authorities they now rubber-stamp the decisions of the party caucus.

Cheshire was run on the basis of offering good salaries, appointing suitable professionals and with only a light rein letting them get on with the job for which they had been trained. That attitude is every-where a thing of the past. The pace of change however has in many authorities outstripped the ability of the organization to adjust to the new relationships required between the paid professionals and the elected members.

4 Reviewing the structure

It is part of the remit of the chief executive to keep the organization of the authority's work under review. Following the reform of local government in 1974, most authorities adopted a pattern of organization of committees and departments loosely based on the recommendations of the Bains Committee, some of which are set out by way of illustration in the Appendix to this chapter. Some councils have made changes since 1974. Whether they have done so or not, every newly appointed chief executive will inherit a pattern devised by others. He will not have the blank sheet of paper and the free hand of those who devised the immediate post-reorganization structure. He may like or dislike what he finds. What principles should guide him in the task reviewing the organization of work?

Changing the people

The first principle is that it is pointless to change the structure if it is the people manning it who are the problem. Change then the people, not the structure. Find him, her or them, something within their competence. Work on it: discuss it frankly with all those concerned, including the trade union representatives. Do not throw your hand in just because it is difficult – as it always is in the public service with its long and valued tradition of job security. Be inventive, but above all do not settle for a structural change unless it solves the 'people' problem.

Local government tends to provide organizational solutions for 'people' problems. One chief architect, for example, may group work according to type of building: all schools to section A, all housing to section B and so on. His successor may opt for a mix of work in sections to give variety and increase interest. In a third reign, the chief architect may prefer a regional pattern so that all work in Area A should go to one section, all work in Area B to another and so on. The arguments over these structural changes proposed by different chief architects might be prolonged. What is reasonably certain is that the changes would not improve the authority's architecture. If it did improve, it would be due to other factors – the leadership, design flair, personal oversight or greater freedom provided by the reigning chief architect. Or the recruitment of some new and abler architects to the department.

The necessary change

Occasionally performance is impeded by structure. An existing service, forming part of the remit of a committee with several services to oversee, may feel itself a cinderella. There may be lack of motiviation among staff. Its bids for resources may be swamped by others at budget time. A change in structure may remove frustration and release latent talents. The change might be to create a subcommittee for the service concerned or more drastically to create another main committee. Alternatively it may be possible to rearrange the business of the committee in such a way that the service in question has a clearer identity, with positive recognition of the status of the officer in charge.

When a new function is taken on, or an existing one is greatly enlarged, the question arises whether to create a new committee for the new or enlarged purpose. No one wishes to proliferate com-mittees, but sometimes the required emphasis and purposefulness cannot be achieved by lumping in the new work within the existing structure. Too much emphasis can be placed on avoiding an increase in the number of main committees. The number of meetings, the size and span of the agenda, the range of interest expected of councillors, must all be taken into account.

NEW LOOK LIBRARIES

Not long after my arrival in Cheshire, I formed the view that the library service was below the standard which might have been expected for a county of Cheshire's size. It was to some extent starved of resources and without the reputation in library circles to attract the best staff. This was the view of the senior regional inspector of the Ministry of Education. It was the view of other county librarians and supported by the comparative statistics published by the County Councils Association. More importantly I found that it was the view of the chairman and vice chairman of the council.

The problem stemmed from the fact that the library service was a subcommittee of the Education Committee. The county librarian's status and salary reflected this subordinate position. Clearly, if the library service were to do better, it had to be prised from education. The structure was inhibiting performance. Only the creation of a new Library Committee with a wider remit was likely to solve the problem. Whilst there was a good measure of agreement on this proposal, the Education Committee mustered enough support for the matter to be referred back, but it was approved on the second occasion.

If the new Committee was to be a success, the council had to create a post of Director of Libraries at a salary which would attract capable applicants, including the existing county librarian. I sought the advice of the City Librarian of Liverpool on this and asked him to assist me in preparing a short list and giving preliminary interviews to those selected – all this being done with the approval of the newly appointed chairman of the committee. There are often casualties when major changes are made and the former county librarian was one such, for he had to accept the post of deputy to the newly appointed director – although at a higher salary than he formerly enjoyed. In interviewing him afterwards I could sense his deep disappointment. Able though he was, he was too much identified with the past to be able to project the new image and do what was required. It is no use embarking on a structural change, without thinking about the people who will man the new organization, for it is they who will determine the success or failure of what is done.

Change for change's sake

No one is likely to embark upon a review programme of committee and departmental organization just for the fun of it – change for change's sake.

There is nevertheless some truth in the slogan 'If it works, it's obsolescent'. Some organizations and some managements achieve success by regular change. There is evidence that human nature responds to change and that it can generate energies and enthusiasm. Structures can become ossified and procedures stagnant. If the scene has been unchanged for many years, the chief executive should consider whether a review should be put in hand with a view to introducing some new patterns. The very fact that a review is being undertaken may have a stimulating effect. If the results may hold promise of savings in cost and shortening of procedures, the support of the leadership at member level should not be difficult to get.

The size of committees

A question which is frequently debated when committees are being reviewed is the correct size of a committee. There seems little objective criteria to answer this question. Certainly the smaller the committee, the less the administrative costs of servicing it and the greater the probability that business will be dealt with expeditiously. In practice, objective criteria will not be applied. There will be certain councillors who must be considered for membership and this will tend to determine the minimum size which can be proposed. The chief executive may have firm views on size but this is an area where members of the authority will reach their own decisions based on a variety of personal and political considerations. There may be some scope for smaller numbers in the less popular committees – with the popular committees like housing, education, social services and planning, there are usually more members wishing to serve than there can be places made available. If one adds in the fact that every authority has a tradition about size of committees, it reinforces the view that this subject is one for the chief executive to take a cautious view about the scope for change.

If proposals for review are to be embarked upon, the areas upon which agreement needs to be reached include:

1 The proportions in which political parties will share the available places: this in turn affects possible sizes, which need to be readily divisible in the agreed shares.

2 The extent to which members' preferences should be a determinant of size. If a committee is popular, should it be larger?

3 Whether it is desirable to have a degree of geographical representation, particularly where the authority's area is large.

It is obvious that these are minefield areas into which the chief executive should only enter if the political leadership has the will and desire to make changes.

COUNCILLORS IN PLENTY

The newly elected councillors in Cheshire in 1965 were not willing to see the county aldermen and long serving councillors hog all the seats on the main committees. Some had as many as 10 committees to serve on. The desire for reform in allocation of committee places provided a useful vehicle for a package of more sweeping reforms of the committee structure, methods of reporting and standing orders governing council business. As part of this package it was agreed to institute a system of members' preferences. This highlighted the problem of finding enough interesting work for all the willing hands. I recall that on one occasion only two people made the Fire Brigade Committee their first choice. One was the chairman and the other a councillor who thought he ought to be chairman. The Fire Brigade is a good example of a service which has but limited scope for member involvement; it is so closely controlled by statutory regulations. It has often seemed to me that most councils are too large for the functions they perform. The importance of the councillor's role is diminished by the absence of rewarding work. Americans who come to Britain on the exchange programme organized by the Society of the Local Authoriy Chief Executives (SOLACE) are uniformly astonished at the size of our councils and committees. There are no doubt some exceptional cases, for example where councillors have much 'constituency' work. But in general it seems a pity that the reduction in numbers of local authorities in 1974 was not matched by as sweeping a reduction in the number of councillors. Fewer and better would be a good precept to follow.

The multipurpose department

The trend since reorganization has been to create conglomerate departments responsible for a range of activities each of which formerly had its own committee and department. This change in organization stemmed from the concept of PPBS, Programming Planning and Budgeting Systems, originating in the United States Navy Department and having a considerable impact on local government in the late 1960s. The concept made many people realize that a traditional budget does not throw up the choices available, indeed may tend to blur and conceal them. If a local authority runs parks, libraries and museums, swimming baths, golf courses, sports halls and other recreational facilities, why not group all these heads of expenditure under the title 'Leisure and Amenities', instead of having them dispersed under separate and discrete budget heads corresponding to the historical committee pattern? (Those who adopted these ideas soon realized the truth of the observation that PPBS may sharpen up the issues, but does not make it any easier to choose. It is a technique of presentation. It does not of itself make it any easier to take decisions on the more clearly perceived options.)

Many of the committees and departments set up in 1974 after reorganization were based upon the concept of programme areas. From most points of view this was a step forward. Budget and spending choices were silhouetted in a new way. The larger remit of the new committees meant more interesting and varied work for members. Provided that the new committee did not proliferate sub-committees, there were opportunities for administrative savings. The larger departments created in this way could provide better career opportunities for staff and better prospects of training, particularly for clerical and administrative staff otherwise condemned to a life of work in a small department, waiting for deadmen's shoes.

It was a fashionable fantasy that to create these larger conglomerate departments was to move into a new, efficient and well-ordered world. In practice there are many problems. If these are not continously worked upon, it may be wiser to be unfashionable and revert to smaller more easily managed units, retaining the programme area concept to settle the budget and for other purposes.

What are the problems which can undermine the apparently solid advantages of the programme area unit? There are three problem areas to which the chief executive should be alive and to which he needs to give attention:

1 motivation and loyalty of the different parts of the whole;

2 control and coordination, especially where the parts are in separate locations;

3 avoidance of creeping fragmentation, the various parts so promisingly brought together, gradually separating in practical working.

Of these the first is the most important. If motivation can be maintained, many of the other problems will not materialize or will be minimized. Many authorities have recognized this, and have retained the former titles so that for example in a leisure department there might be a chief librarian, a parks superintendent (or director) and a sports centre director. These three will have separate professional backgrounds and training; different outlooks and staffing considerations. Parks have manual staff; libraries have large numbers of staff who wish to qualify as librarians; sports centres need bar and catering staff, athletic coaches, sub-managers, and so forth. To provide one chief officer, who can command the support and loyalty of such different groups is no easy task. Yet without positive leadership, the expected benefits will not materialize. Libraries will not mount exhibitions (or even lending points) in sports centres; the parks department will not use libraries and sports halls for selling their services; and staff at all levels will not find it easy to move sideways from their own departmental straitjacket.

Similar problems can readily be seen to arise with departments of technical services, usually comprising architecture, engineering and planning, or the newly fashionable property departments comprising valuation, architecture, land management and town planning. The choice of a person to head such a directorate is a difficult one. A 'generalist' manager of a technical services department is likely to be regarded by the professionals as a charlatan. Yet there are few professionals who can offer all or even most of the specialisms, there being some architect/planners and some chartered surveyors/ planners but not many others with dual or multiple qualifications. Whatever the professional discipline of the man at the top, all the other professionals will feel that they and their work have been placed in a subordinate position. So the man at the top needs extreme sensibility and a breadth of approach if he is to obtain from the combined department the benefits expected of it. Separation of location serves to compound all these problems. If the staffs are all physically separate they will not get to know each other. There will be a pretence of a joint department, existing on paper, but not in geographical reality. No chief executive should recommend the creation of a multipurpose department, if there are no prospects of bringing most of the staff into reasonable proximity to each other within a measurable space of time.

THE PAIN OF CHANGE

Attending a North-Western civic lunch in connection with the 1974 reorganization I sat next to a lady councillor whose lifelong enthusiasm had been the library service. She was describing the new order of things in which she had lost her chairmanship because her committee had been merged into a larger new Leisure and Recreation Committee. 'How do you feel about all this?' I asked. 'Ee' she replied in broad Lancashire, 'ah feel cut off at knees'. Change can be painful.

Making the multipurpose department work

What can the chief executive do to ease the problems these large committees and departments can create?

1 The selection of the head of the department is all important. The chief executive must be sensitive to the inter-professional jealousies which can arise and see that members appreciate them. The departmental head will need support. At the same time, the important sectional heads must feel that they too can have access to the chairman of the committee and to the chief executive.

2 The titles of the posts of sectional head and their status must be such as to satisfy the needs for professional recognition of the

postholder. If the sectional head does not have a subcommittee of his own to report to, it is important that he has full scope to present his matters to the main committee.

3 If subcommittees are created to cover some of the special interests comprised within the remit of the main committee, the terms of reference of subcommittees and main committee must be well defined. If a planning subcommittee and a roads subcommittee are to operate under the aegis of a planning and transportation committee, the chief executive must ensure that everyone understands the extent of delegation to the subcommittee, and the matters of principle and joint involvement which are to be reserved to the main committee. If such a main committee is intended to pull together the strands of thought on a problem affecting two disciplines, for example the town planning and highway aspects of an inner relief road, it is essential that there are good working relationships at officer level. The chief executive must ensure that the main committee is not presented with two reports pulling in opposite directions. He is unlikely to be able to do this without some formal machinery to run through matters intended to come before the main committee. At a regular meeting for this purpose, many areas of possible disagreement between departments can be ironed out, leaving the committee to decide upon matters which may remain in dispute.

4 Better promotion prospects for clerical and administrative staff serving a larger organization, are unlikely to come about on their own simply by reliance upon staff applying for vacancies in the normal way. Staff should be brought together for training purposes. Secondments should be arranged, so that a promising administrator can work in another section and show his worth. Seminars for professional staff, embracing people of different professional disciplines, can be arranged to consider a subject or subjects of common interest and concern. The chief executive should discuss with the departmental head these and other possibilities of welding the conglomerate department together.

During the last war it was observed that prisoners hung on grimly to their nationalities and tended to speak and fraternize only with those from their own country of origin. Something like this seems to happen with professional disciplines. Planners remain planners. Engineers remain engineers. Librarians remain librarians. Parks superintendents remain park superintendents. On paper they may be planning/transportation, or leisure/amenities or land agent/architects' staff, but the paper organization will not break down the barriers which background, training and professionalism create. There can be considerable advantages, as has been pointed out, in basing staff organization on programme areas. However, those who do not recognize the barriers which exist, who have not thought of ways in which they can be gradually broken down and of the effort which will have to be deployed to do so, should not embark upon creating combined departments. Just because a radical solution is rejected, this should not prevent the chief executive from securing the benefits of joint working by other means. The starting point of these may well be a regular programmed meeting (perhaps three times a year) between the chief executive and the heads of departments within the programme area. One of these would be to discuss the budgets of the departments on a programme area basis. Joint working groups could be established to look at some areas where cooperation could achieve results. A joint training programme could be established and, as part of it, all staff made to realize their contribution to the programme area. Ways of improving mobility of staff between departments could be explored. The programme area concept has much to commend it. It can be used to bring together those who might otherwise work in relative isolation. Some simple measures may be able to produce most of the benefits without taking on board the trauma of radical reorganization.

Appendix 4.1

See pages 38–40, figures 1–3 representing in outline the departmental structure of non-metropolitan county and district authorities, and page 41 which lists terms of reference for a policy and resources committee. These are extracted from the report of the committee on *The New Local Authorities; Management and Structure* published by Her Majesty's Stationery Office 1972

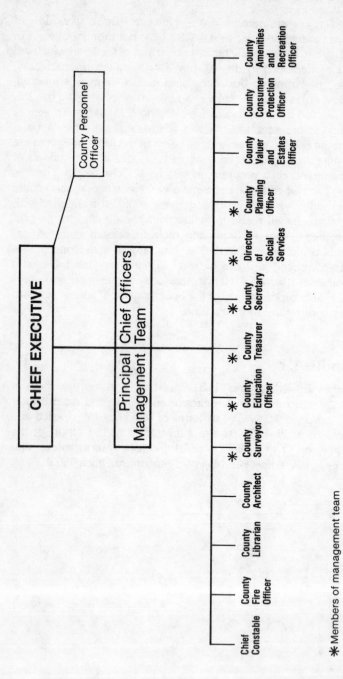

Figure 1 – Departmental structure A – Non-metropolitan county

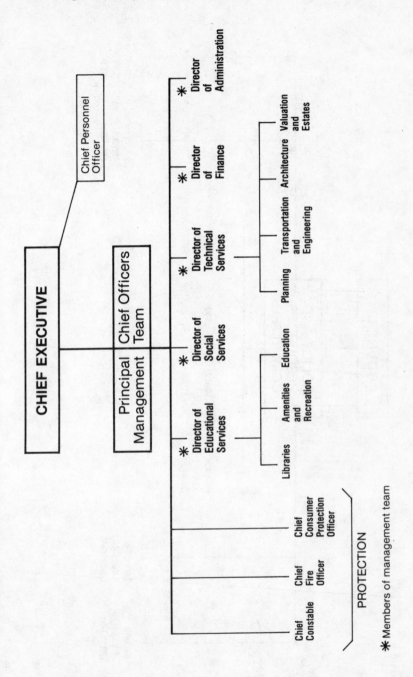

Figure 2 – Departmental structure B – Non-metropolitan county

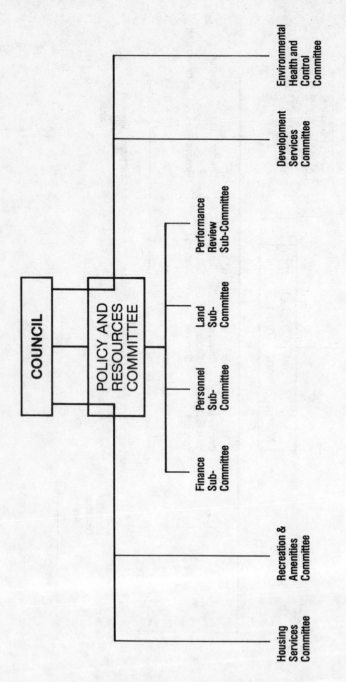

Figure 3 – Committee structure B – Non-metropolitan district

TERMS OF REFERENCE FOR A POLICY AND RESOURCES COMMITTEE

1 To guide the Council in the formulation of its corporate plan of objectives and priorities, and for this purpose to recommend to the council such forward programmes and other steps as may be necessary to achieve those objectives, either in whole or in part, during specific time spans. For this purpose to consider the broad social and economic needs of the authority and matters of comprehensive importance to the area including the contents of structure plans. To advise the Council generally as to its financial and economic policies.

2 Without prejudice to the duties and responsibilities of the programme committees, to review the effectiveness of all the Council's work and the standards and levels of service provided. To identify the need for new services and to keep under review the necessity for existing ones.

3 To submit to the Council concurrent reports with the programme committees upon new policies or changes in policy formulated by such committees, particularly those which may have significant impact upon the corporate plan or the resources of the Council.

4 To be responsible for allocating and controlling the financial, manpower and land resources of the Council.

5 To ensure that the organisation and management processes of the council are designed to make the most effective contribution to the achievement of the Council's objectives. To keep them under review in the light of changing circumstances, making recommendations as necessary for change in either the committee or departmental structure, or the distribution of functions and responsibilities.

6 To be concerned together with the appropriate programme committee in the appointment of Heads of Departments and any Deputies.

5 The budget and finance

Of all the decisions taken by a local authority none is more important than the budget. It both sets future policy and reflects past policy decisions. It goes without saying that the chief executive should be fully involved in every aspect of budget formulation. If he is a former treasurer he must resist the temptation to be both chief executive and director of finance. Their roles are (or should be) different and one man should not try and play both – though the few who hold both appointments will have to do so. The chief executive and the treasurer should work together, in agreeing the procedures and timetable to be followed; in presenting the choices open to councillors; and in ensuring that advice as to the options available is agreed by chief officers concerned.

Procedures

The central financing of local government has introduced such complex concepts that few people understand them in detail. Older hands may look back wistfully at such easily understood systems as the percentage grant or the early simplicity of the rate support grant. There has over the past decade been a steady sophistication of the machinery of central government control. One result has been the growth of 'creative accounting' with presentational devices and the treatment of receipts, balances, capital expenditure and other matters designed to circumvent the effects of the centrally imposed rules. The principal result has however been that in most local authorities there is one man or more likely a group of men whose year-round task is the budget. The group may have one of several titles in common usage, but their task will not vary much in principle between one council and another. The danger is that the budget becomes a sort of religion, with the budget team serving as its high priests, jealously guarding their secrets from the uninitiated. Ideas and procedures designed to illuminate the choices open to members may be over-elaborated by the budget team so that the paper work grows and the timetable starts earlier and earlier. The well intentioned enthusiasm and fervour of the budget team may actually increase incomprehensibility.

The chief executive and the director of finance must guard against any growth in budget formulation activity which tends to isolate those who know the facts about a service from the high priests who express service requirements in budget terms. Sophistication tends to breed further sophistication. Because budget papers are impressively complicated and are fuller than the previous year does not mean that a better budget is being constructed. The budget is a necessary and important activity. But the budget must not be allowed to take on a life of its own. It exists to serve rather than to be served. Its complexity demands specialist knowledge and attention. However the aim must be to simplify, to reduce, to shorten, to start nearer the budget period and to widen the circle of those who understand it outside the specialist group. To achieve those objectives will require continuous attention from the chief executive and the finance director.

Policy options

Many local authorities have made changes in the format of their budgets in order to highlight the policy options open to the council. These changes have been one of the results of the consideration of ideas about PPBS (Planning Programming and Budgeting Systems). Even if the council's organizational structure has not been altered so as to group related activities in a single department it is perfectly possible to prepare a budget statement by programme areas in addition to conventional estimating under committee responsibilities and heads. Parks, sports halls, museums, libraries and subsidies to the arts, for example, may not fall within the ambit of a single committee. This need not prevent the formulation of a statement of the use of resources on leisure and recreation – possibly a separate statement because a budget for expenditure control purposes may have to be presented on a committee expenditure basis. Presenting the budget so as to illuminate policy options for expenditure – or for cuts in expenditure – does entail additional work, most pronounced in the year in which new formats are established, but continuing year by year thereafter. One of the depressing aspects of this additional work is that it does not make it any easier to choose between the various possibilities presented by programme analysis. 'To govern is

to choose' wrote Montesquieu. Choice for members or officers is
never easy. There is a point at which elaboration ceases to be helpful,
in the sense that it is unlikely to result in earlier or better decisions. With
this qualification there is no doubt that analysis of past or proposed
expenditure by programme areas is desirable – indeed many would
say essential.

Subject analysis

Analysis by subject is also essential – an across-the-board look at some
element of expenditure which is to be found scattered in different parts of
a budget constructed on an operational control basis. If this is not already
done on a systematic basis the chief executive should discuss the
possibilities with the director of finance and see if some areas can be
selected for analysis either as part of, or outside the budgetary process.
Some examples, perhaps obvious, may illustrate what is meant.

1 Insurance premiums are often apportioned among the various
spending committees. How much is spent in total and on what
categories of risk? What is the claims experience? Could some risks be
carried by the council to a greater extent than hitherto?

2 Cleaning of council premises is often split in a traditional budget
between committees and again between wages, salaries, materials
and equipment. What is the global total and the costs per square foot
or metre? Are there uniform standards and who sets them?

3 Most services require transport. What is the cost per mile for similar
vehicles? Is there any policy of standardization on vehicle types? Is
there a replacement policy? What are the maintenance arrangements
and unit costs? (The Audit Commission's report on Transport,
November 1984 would be relevant here).

4 The manager of particular council premises frequently has a right to
order first aid repairs. Is the current limit realistic? How much is spent in
this way? Do different departments have different rules, and is this
justified?

Inter-authority comparison

For many years a great deal of information has been made available
about the comparative expenditure of different authorities, for example, those produced by the Chartered Institute of Public Finance
and Accountancy, the profile of the authority prepared by the Audit

Commission, and the manpower returns of the Local Authorities Conditions of Service Advisory Board. Everyone knows that it is difficult to make valid comparisons between one authority and another simply on the basis of statistical information. Anyone who has worked with several local authorities will know of factors which the statistics cannot reveal. Nevertheless comparative expenditure tables and the Audit Commission's profile of the authority provide material on which the chief executive can ask questions, either as part of the scrutiny of budgets or otherwise. Higher than average expenditure on administration, for example, deserves a question and an answer. It may be that the administration is better and more purposeful, and its higher cost may be offset by securing better value for money. Above average administration costs may be because the service is more locally responsive. There may be an area organization which in the council's opinion gives the public a better service. However a decision to be locally responsive taken at a time of plenty may need review when expenditure is being cut back. Questions should, of course not be confined simply to those facets of expenditure where the council seems to spend more per head or per case than other similar authorities. The comparative information may indicate areas where there is a noticeable gap in service provision, where ratepayers clearly get a poorer response than those in neighbouring authorities. There is often a historical reason for these inequalities. The enthusiasms of chairmen of committees, and of chief and senior officers may lead to an emphasis and development of some parts of their service at the expense of others. Similarly a belief that certain types of expenditure are less valuable than others or that provision for certain needs is unjustifiable may distort an authority's expenditure from the norm. There are fashions, too, about what provision is desirable and at given moments particular theories hold sway.

It is almost inevitable that the head of a department and its senior staff will feel defensive about the department's performance. Comparative statistical information may be brushed aside as not telling the whole story or as being unreliable or simply because an effort is needed to use it intelligently. The chief executive must encourage an open-minded approach, in which questions are not resented but welcomed. He can promote this attitude of mind by personally welcoming questions which impinge on his own activities or responsibilities. If he is seen to accept that his job is to serve the public better and not to safeguard a private empire or vested self-interest, others will be more readily persuaded to accept the value of an inquisitorial approach. The ideal and ultimate position is one in which those who know the answers have begun to ask themselves the questions, using comparative information as merely one tool to achieving better performance.

If the chief executive is not to ask naive questions he will need help from those with some firsthand day-to-day knowledge of the department concerned – either at administrative, financial, legal or internal audit level. He will also have to carry the director of finance with him in his thinking because much of the information is provided through his department. The director of finance in particular will be aware of the possibilities of misinterpretation of information, as a result of difficulties of agreeing a common base for its provision or the like.

FOLLOWING THE FASHION

Few would deny that there are fashions in expenditure – and indeed in ways of reducing it.

There was a time when most police forces in the country were making strenuous efforts to equip themselves as fast as possible with Panda cars. This Home Office led innovation (which was extremely good for the motor car industry) was portrayed as the answer to the modern criminal. Yet within a decade chief officers of police were extolling the virtues of the police officer on the beat. Panda cars no doubt have an important part to play in crime prevention, but their introduction was the fashion of the day, which only a very strong-minded police authority would have dared resist. The great objective in education for years was to improve the pupil teacher ratio. It was the fashion of the day to make this the touchstone of progress. It took time before educationalists began to ask themselves when the process of reduction should stop, and whether the money spent in this process might yield better results for pupils if applied elsewhere. Currently the fashionable thinking about saving ratepayers money is privatization. It surely has a place, but like other panaceas is not a complete answer.

Looking back, I think that I went along with much of what at the time was fashionable. Age and experience tends to produce scepticism, no bad thing provided it is not the product of a shut mind. One of the tasks of those at the top must be to challenge the accepted and conventional wisdom.

Value for money

Good local government officers have always been concerned about value for money. Where there has been such concern, the most expensive has not been purchased on the assumption that it must be the best value, nor has the lowest tender been accepted on the assumption that the cheapest must be the best. The good officer has acted with the prudence he would display if he were spending his own, not the ratepayers', money. He knows that it is not necessary to over-elaborate the specification for a vehicle or a piece of equipment. He knows that low first cost is often offset by high maintenance expenditure. He knows that care is always needed in deciding what is required, and how to obtain satisfactory prices, within the authority's Standing Orders.

Statutory force has been given to good practice by the requirement in the Local Government Finance Act 1982 that an auditor must be satisfied that there are proper arrangements for securing economy, efficiency and effectiveness in the use of resources by the authority. The chief executive will be very much concerned to see that throughout his authority there are good management practices. He will do what he can to produce the right climate of opinion so that staff at all levels do not go on ordering goods services or work just because they were ordered the year before, but re-examine their requirements critically. Is it needed at all? Is it needed to this specification? Much can be done by example, precept and training to get across at every level of performance the need to secure value for money not only in the supply of goods and services, but in the utilization of resources, both material and manpower.

The Standing Orders relating to contracts of the authority should be reviewed to see whether they hinder rather than help forward the concept of value for money. Standing Orders are primarily concerned to prevent fraudulent collusion between a contractor on the one hand and councillors or officials on the other. They may be admirable for this purpose, but too inflexible to allow the authority easily to accept what a prudent man of business would decide to be the best offer. If they are too inflexible, the standing orders should be changed.

Besides inculcating the right approach to value for money, the chief executive should ensure that he and his authority use the tools fashioned for this purpose by the Audit Commission. Set up in 1982, the Commission not only appoints the auditors for local authorities in England and Wales but carries out studies to define good practice in a particular field. Each study results in a published report, an audit guide and a detailed manual for those interested in the service in question. By establishing a good practice yardstick, the reports allow individual authorities (and their auditor) to identify areas in which improved value for money could be obtained. The chief executive should read the reports himself so as to be able to play a positive role in implementing the good ideas resulting from the study. These special studies, of which a few will be done each year, supplement and complement what is contained in the Audit Commission's

Handbook on Improving Economy Efficiency and Effectiveness, an admirable publication designed to stimulate thinking, and focus attention on areas likely to yield results. There is, indeed, no shortage of reading matter, including the publication of case studies by the Society of Local Authority Chief Executives and the Chartered Institute of Public Finance and Accountancy.

LEADING THE FIELD

At one of the day seminars for chief officers, we had a talk from the head of the management services division of Imperial Chemical Industries. I recall only one thing he said. 'We have found that it is expensive to be out in front'. A little later I was in Portland, Oregon, looking at the new computer based system of issuing motor taxation discs. After two years hard work the system was nearly as fast as the old manual system. There had been many problems. I was taking some notes as the party walked round the hardware. Observing my apparent interest, a white coated civil servant came up beside me and out of the corner of his mouth said 'Sir, I would let someone else pioneer this, if I were you'. Local government needs some pioneers. But if money is short, you need not pioneer everything yourself.

Social and Economic trends

The chief executive must find the time to be informed about the broad economic issues and framework at national level against which his own authority's budget must be set. A basic discipline in law or even accountancy does not always promote an interest in these wider issues. Many chief executives have never perused the annual Blue Book on national income and expenditure, let alone kept one in a desk drawer, or read any of the illuminating and useful papers produced regularly by the National Economic Development Office and government departments. To some extent this is pardonable because the size and complexity of the various government white papers on public expenditure make demands on the time of the chief executive and may crowd out other apparently less essential reading. This should not be confined to simple 'economic' matters like production figures and employment numbers, but embrace social trends as well. The style and scope of local authority provision is bound in the longer term to be largely determined by socio-economic factors. The growth in home ownership, in ownership of motor cars, washing machines, refrigerators, colour television; the pattern of accommodation of young people after marriage, spending patterns of different age groups; demographic patterns showing the growth in the old and young; all these and many more must affect the nature and extent of council housing, the provision of home helps, of old people's homes or services, of leisure and recreational services, of ideas about policing and of roads and transportation policies, to name but a few. Local authorities have on the whole been slow to recognize changes in social behaviour and expectations, and have maintained policies the justification of which has passed. Some housing authorities were, for example, planning to build overspill estates in the late 1960s when those on the housing waiting lists were unwilling to take older accommodation offered to them, so that there was an embarrassment of numerous unlet older properties. The desire of young marrieds to have council accommodation, a basic feature of the early post-war years, was changing both in the size of the demand and the expectation as to what should be provided. Single parent families were also becoming of increasing importance as potential tenants of council accommodation. Housing authorities were slow to detect trends like these.

To take another example, the relentless growth in car ownership must affect traditional views about transport and parking policies, out of town shopping facilities, rural buses, patterns of employment and other areas where the authority's policies may reflect the thinking of ten years ago, or even earlier.

The chief executive cannot be an expert in everything. A study of socio-economic factors is a study in itself, requiring training and experience. The chief executive can do a great deal however to keep himself informed, to widen his horizons, to broaden the perspective of his thinking. In a large authority he should try and recruit some staff with an economics background so that somewhere in the organization – in the planning department, the finance department, the corporate planning unit or in the chief executive's own staff unit if he has one – there can be an input of a sort which has often been lacking in the past. Wherever the economist works, he should be able to talk to the chief executive and keep him informed.

LOOKING AHEAD

The report by the Central Policy Review Staff on Population and the Social Services (1977), alerted me to two areas of concern. The first was the increasing number of school leavers who would come onto the job market in the early 1980s. This was the bulge in the birthrate in the 1960s working its way inexorably forward through the schools (where it necessitated a huge building programme) to school leaving age, when more jobs were clearly needed for those not going on to further education.

The second was the reverse of the coin, the falling numbers on school rolls in the 1980s and 1990s.

Consideration of the need for jobs led to the creation of a small officers group, the Employment Board, centred on the Planning Department. Once we had cleared our minds as to what we might be able to do, we asked the Policy and Resources Committee to set up a new subcommittee to take on this important new remit.

The fall in school rolls raised the spectre of school closures a difficult political area for councillors. The Director of Education and I arranged for all councillors to attend if they wished a day seminar to learn the facts and consider the implications. These extended beyond the education department itself to such topics as the future size of the architects department, central supplies, and other services closely related to education.

The point of the story is that without my personal reading of the CPRS research study, these initiatives would have taken longer to develop. People are so much immersed in today's job that there is often no time given to look ahead.

Some practical problems

This is not the place to produce a treatise on budgeting practices and procedures. Most local authorities have developed their own systems and formats. Whilst the chief executive may be able to suggest improvements he will have to work largely with what has traditionally been provided, assuming of course that it is competent and in its own way acceptable. What follows is an attempt to indicate matters which need to be taken into the reckoning when thinking about the budget and the chief executive's role in relation to it. They are matters more of psychology and human relations than techniques or financial knowledge.

1 Budgets are rarely approved without cuts. Even in the less stringent conditions of the 1960s and 1970s, estimates from departments to their committees were rarely approved without question. It follows that those who produce the estimates for approval expect to lose some items before approval is given. This more often than not leads to items being included which the author of the request expects to lose in the budgetary process. Or a series of items may be pitched on the high side to allow some fat for subsequent slimming. The chief executive will certainly be aware of this syndrome. But he needs to acquire a feel for those departments or sections where there may be a more cynical and less honest approach. Departments vary, with some by tradition treating the

budget as a contest between themselves and the central scrutinizing group or committee.

2 Some elements in the budget may be presented as forming part of a mystique which no one should dare challenge. The priorities for building repairs; the budget for computer development; the purchase of specialized equipment or machinery; the ratio of staff to pupils or children in care – these and similar items may be, in a sense, withdrawn from normal scrutiny. The chief executive should take a lead in ensuring that no part of the budget is sacrosanct or incapable of challenge or inquiry. The assumptions on which the estimates have been based need to be established and critically examined. The 'expert' should never be allowed to throw up a smoke screen of technical jargon. If he is a good expert he will be pleased to try and explain his thinking to the non-expert. Every now and then the non-expert will, by the very process of explanation, cause some matter to be reconsidered. The generalist should have a proper regard for the specialist. He should not seek to impose his amateur views on the professional. Equally, he should not regard himself as muzzled, just because the issue has a strong element of specialism in it, whether the issue is a budget issue or arises at some other time.

3 Budgets are, or should be, about policies, priorities and options. Some councils, particularly those with large political majorities, may have clear policies which can be expressed in the budget. The first budget will reflect the expressed wishes of the majority party, even if reductions have later to be made to meet government spending targets or to reduce the rate level to what is considered to be politically acceptable. Other councils do not give detailed guidance but may work within some general statement such as 'containing the rate demand at last year's level in real terms'. The chief executive should realize that he and the departmental heads are poor in-struments for taking political decisions. Genuine political decision requires some background of political philosophy and some political objectives. The politician may believe in subsidizing bus services; or think that roads are well maintained and can stand some lean years; or believe in the need for cheap recreation at a time of mass un-employement; or be determined to make the number of school places fit the lower number of school children – to give but a few examples. A budget can reflect these convictions. The chief ex-ecutive is a trained administrator as are the heads of departments. The administrator seeks for compromise, for a middle way which will not upset too many. If officers are left to construct budgets without objectives or to suggest savings, the result will almost inevitably be a bland mixture of trade-offs and compromises between the various services. Traditional patterns of expenditure · will probably be maintained. Hard decisions will not be taken, because that implies a political judgement.

The chief executive should be wary of accepting for himself or his chief officers 'political' responsibility for the budget. Means must be found of making councillors (who can also find hard decisions unpalatable) reach the conclusions on the contentious parts of the budget estimates. There are many ways in which this can be done; for example reductions in expenditure may be given a priority rating by departmental heads. This could be either a simple preference scale or based on some agreed objective criteria, for example the effects on manpower, or service levels, or methods of working. Officers can and should illuminate the choices open to the council and try and ensure that the necessary choices are made. The administrator's solution like 'cut three percent across the board' should be adopted only as a last resort. The chief executive is in a unique position to give impartial advice if called upon to do so. He need not shrink from giving it. Yet he should realize the limitations of the administration when called upon to do work which should be done by the elected representatives.

AFTER THE DECISION

The Budget is the time at which many decisions are taken at least in principle. On the whole councils do not find it easy to take decisions. There is a demand for more and more information, which is often no more than a substitute for decision taking. Local Government in consequence is good at producing analyses, evaluations, cost benefit appraisals and so forth. I can recall the endless papers I wrote and the debates upon them as to whether Berkshire's new Shire Hall should be built in Reading City Centre or on an available site on the outskirts. The truth is that either would have done: and the irony is that it was eventually built on neither. The proposal for a new and costly central workshop in Cheshire was referred back some three or four times by the council for further studies and reports. Costs rose inexorably during these deferments (for this occurred at the height of the period of inflation of building costs in the early 1970s) so that each new batch of savings was negatived by inflation.

Because decision taking is often a hard and prolonged process, it often seems to me that it results in a form of exhaustion, with the result that implementation of the decision gets less attention than it deserves. Implementation is not carried out in the glare of publicity which attends the decision. It is incremental and is rarely dramatic. It may therefore be left to be carried out at lower levels than it should be, whilst the principal actors get ready for immersion in a new set of appraisals, option analyses and other studies. Decision taking by private enterprise, as I have seen it, is often less well informed than in the public service. But it is infinitely quicker and there is then total commitment at all levels from the top down to seeing the decision through to successful finality.

When taking decisions, it is well to be on guard against over optimism in the assumptions put forward to councillors. Experience shows that savings from installing new office or other equipment are but slowly realized, because the difficulty of staff retraining is underestimated. Experience shows that it always takes longer to open or close service points because of difficulties over the premises, the staff, or the equipment. Experience shows that to join two or more units together in the expectation that overheads will be shared and economies effected, can be a longer and more difficult process than the authors of the scheme have expected.

Assumptions about expected results need to take account of experience. These assumptions affect the credibility of those who put their name to them: it may be safer to err on the side of pessimism.

6 Politics, ethics and the hung council

Party politics are not a new thing in local government. Some councils have been run on party political lines for half a century or more. What is new is that nearly all councils throughout the length and breadth of the land are now run in this way. The importance which party politics play will vary from one council to another, but there are now only a handful which proclaim themselves as non-political or independent. The reorganization of 1974 accelerated the growth of a tendency to political grouping within the ranks of elected members. Some at least of the problems which party politics give rise to may be due to the speed with which the change has occurred. Councils without any history or tradition of working on political lines began in 1974 to do so, not in any tentative or embryonic way, but on lines similar to those with developed party political systems.

Another change occurred in 1974 which has a bearing on the question of party politics in local government. This was the acceptance by nearly all authorities of the concept of a chief executive, someone appointed and recognized as the head of the paid administration as opposed to the earlier concept of someone who was *primus inter pares* or first among equals. Town clerks and clerks of councils had, prior to 1974, often acted as chief executives. What was new was not so much the change in status as the change in the expectations of councillors. They expected something more than a legal/secretarial, coordinator/administrator activity. The higher profile demanded of the newly created chief executive in itself raised new problems as to the relations of the office holder with the political parties.

These relations are often compared to those between senior civil servants and their ministers. Certainly there are similarities. Both the civil servant and his counterpart in local government are expected to be impartial, neutral and non-political and to serve the interests of the political masters of the day to the best of their ability. Both expect to stay in office whatever changes may occur to the political parties at election time. Both have a high degree of personal responsibility and accountability. Over the civil servant is the minister who takes responsibility in Parliament for his department, and over the local government officer is the committee or the council, answerable to the electorate for the administration of the affairs of the local authority.

Helpful though this analogy with the civil service is in some ways, it tends to obscure some major differences.

The first is that in law, the chief executive and chief officers are appointed and paid by the council and must be answerable and accountable to the council as a whole. There is no separation between a legislature and an executive, as in central government, the council being an uneasy amalgam of both. A debate in council may have some of the features of a debate in Parliament, but the measures being discussed have been prepared not by an independent executive, but by some microcosm of the council itself, in the shape of a committee or subcommittee. The chief executive and chief officers serve and advise both committees and the council. They do not have the simple loyalty of the top civil servant to his minister, or the civil servant's ability, as a matter of convention, virtually to disregard the Opposition. The local government chief is working in a differently structured organization and rules applicable to central government will not necessarily translate into local government terms.

The truth of the matter is that local authorities are not well structured for the emphatic and positive party political method of working of today. It is easy to see that a structure of councillors working in council and committees, with an officer administration both advising and executing, need cause no problem of relationships if all the councillors are individuals accepting loyalty only to those who elected them. Decisions will be taken according to the view formed at the time by the majority of the individual councillors in committee or council and in the light of any advice tendered by the paid officials. In this method of working (which obtained in many councils prior to reorganization) the chief officials had to relate to groups of councillors in committee, to chairmen of committees and to the council as a whole. As with all human organizations there was likely to be one preeminent councillor, one leader (often the chairman) with whom a special relationship had to be nurtured. Yet overall, the responsibility was to the council as a whole and to its committees.

On such a basically non-political structure, it was still possible to superimpose something of a party political nature without creating problems of relationships between the paid administration and the elected members. Councillors might for example stand for election under political labels, yet meet rarely in political groups. Voting was more likely to be according to individual conscience than party diktat. Or there might be a more positive approach with party groups meeting before the main meetings of the council, to settle chairmanships and occasional matters of contention, but leaving members considerable freedom to decide matters coming before them in committee according to their own judgement.

In such modestly developed systems of political working, it was still possible for each official to say 'I owe my duty to the council as a whole and to its committees' and still be effective.

But what if some of the committees are composed exclusively of members of one party? What if all the business in committee has already been decided by councillors meeting in their party political groups beforehand? In councils where there are these intensive methods of political working (and they are common enough) the question is whether the chief executive can take refuge in the historical position and still be effective. Of course the law is the law. The chief executive cannot legally be faulted if he says 'I am appointed and paid by the council: I owe my duty to the council as a whole'. Yet he is likely to be faulted by his council if he is unable to build some sort of bridge to span the gap between the law and the reality. The reality is that many important matters are now settled outside the committee room and the council chamber. If there is no machinery for communication between the chief executive and chief officers on the one hand and political masters on the other, one of the traditional roles of the paid administration, evaluation and advice on policy options, will diminish or disappear.

It is a matter of regret that when all political parties have decided consciously or unconsciously, to work in this more assertive political style, so little thought has been given by them to the need to establish robust conventions governing the relations between the parties and the paid staff. Maybe it is too early to do this. Different models are being developed in different authorities. Some chief executives would argue that a single model is in any case impossible or undesirable.

WRITTEN CONVENTIONS

I always considered that there were advantages in having some ground rules to govern the relations between the political parties themselves and their relations to the chief executive and chief officers. Some of my colleagues believed that it was better to play it by ear, but for my part I saw advantages in having a written score however brief upon which the extempore passages could be built.

In 1974, conscious of the increasing politicization of the council scene, I circulated a draft of some principles for consideration by the two principal groups on the council. With amendments it was finally agreed and is reproduced as Appendix 1 to this chapter. It was a simple document prepared with the object of alerting the political parties to some of the problems of running on hard political lines rather than the 'country gentleman' approach which had characterized affairs on the council for quarter of a century and which permitted for example a chairmanship or vice-chairmanship being held by a member of the titular Opposition. What is more interesting than the original is the version in Appendix 2, an elaboration to meet the problems of a 'hung' council with three party groups all, in a sense, of equal power. This Appendix is referred to in the pages dealing with the problems of hung councils later in this chapter.

Yet giving full credit for the need for pragmatism, some principles seem to be needed to guide relationships during this formative period. The chief executive is well advised to have discussions with the leaders of the various parties after an election (particularly where power changes hands or where there are many new councillors) to try and establish some local conventions for the areas which cause practical difficulty. What follows is an attempt to outline some of those areas and to discuss the principles which might apply and to comment generally upon them.

1 The chief executive's independence of the political parties should be unquestionable. There should be no difference between his position in this respect from that of a senior civil servant. All political parties should accept this at national level; but until they do, the Society of Local Authority Chief Executives and the Chief Officers' Societies should assert the position publicly on behalf of their respective members. To assert the neutrality of the chief executive and chief officers is not to deny the need for acute political awareness on their part. But there is a clear difference between political awareness and political commitment.

2 It should be accepted that, for the efficient working of the authority, the chief executive will have to cultivate a special working relationship with the majority party/parties' leadership. The way this special relationship will be developed will vary from one authority to another, and will probably vary over a period even within the same authority. The chief executive, until national conventions and practices are established, will be well advised to tell the minority parties what he intends to do and why he wishes to do it. The same principles hold good for departmental heads.

3 Everyone must understand that there is still validity in the concept that the chief executive owes a duty to the council as a whole. This principle is not dead. It may well be inadequate as a basis for the stance of the chief executive in today's politically oriented councils. Yet its existence makes for one of the major differences with the position of the top civil servant. The latter fulfils his duty by informing his minister. The chief executive cannot simply inform the majority party; he must inform the council. If, for example, legal counsel had advised that a contemplated action was unlawful, the chief executive and chief legal officer could not simply acquiesce in such a view being suppressed or known only by some of the councillors. It would clearly be their duty to ensure that the whole council were aware that the opinion had been given. An opinion as to the legality of proposed action is but one example of a general rule. The chief executive has a duty to see that the council consider material facts within his knowledge before they enter into any burdensome commitment – for example penalty clauses in a contract, hidden extras to a dis-closed purchase price, or the possibility of onerous future liabilities. There is a duty too to ensure that the council as a whole, and not just the majority party, are informed as to the consequences of policies which they may wish to adopt. All this does not mean that a chief executive should be obstructionist or raise pedantic issues which a broader approach might disregard. Common sense is needed. Many chief executives will not experience problems as to where their duty lies. Some with very assertive political leadership may have many. The point which needs to be emphasized is that there is a residual duty to the council as a whole, which politicians must accept. On rare occasions this may mean that the chief executive will have courageously to climb out on a limb hoping that the political axemen will spare the tree.

4 Because the chief executive is the servant of the council and not the majority party, he cannot ignore the minority party in the way that a senior civil servant can as a matter of convention largely ignore the Opposition. The individual councillor is entitled, unless his motive is improper, to see council documents and to receive infor-mation about council business and proceedings where he has 'a need to know'. It is usual therefore to provide for all members of any party without question:

a assistance in framing notices of motion or written questions to be put at council meetings (although here it must not appear that the chief executive is actively helping the Opposition to be effective)

b information which is readily available in the form required by the councillor concerned from published minutes, reports, abstracts and so forth.

Problems mainly arise where information is asked for which would entail considerable research. It is one thing to look out and copy some existing material which covers most of the ground of inquiry. It is quite another to have staff extracting matter from different sources to produce answers to the questions asked. In such cases, the majority leadership should be asked for approval to the work being undertaken. If this is not forthcoming, the enquirer should be reminded of any rights he may have under Standing Orders to put down written questions. These often give a right to the chairman concerned to decline to answer but such a refusal is a political and not an administrative one.

If there are no conventions in the authority as to the chief executive's responsibilities to the minority parties and to individual councillors it may well be a sensible precaution for him to inform the majority leader of any requests for advice on notices of motion, or for information other than requests on day-to-day routine or minor matters.

5 Finally there is the question of attendance at meetings of political groups. A decade ago it would have been heresy to suggest that such attendance might be permissible. Today a significant number of chief executives believe that such attendance is not only permissible, but desirable or even essential. How else to influence affairs in a world where all important decisions are reached at private meetings of one party, as they are in some local authorities? This is a powerful argument and it may have to be accepted. There *may* be no other way. In some cases, however, it may be possible for the chief executive and his chief officer colleagues to provide their input by regularly briefing two or three political leaders as to the effects of various policy options (it is preferable for oral briefings to be given to two councillors rather than to a single party representative to avoid misunderstanding as to what was in fact said). Oral briefings can be supplemented by written material. If the desired input can be achieved in this way it is easier for the chief executive to be (and to be seen to be) politically independent. Regular consultation with and briefing of the political leadership is no new thing and in some authorities it may be all that is needed. It can be supplemented by occasional attendance at party group meetings on very important subjects such as the annual budget where the majority party as a whole may wish to be able to ask questions of the chief executive and the treasurer so that a briefing session for chairmen only is regarded as inadequate. Nevertheless there are authorities where the chief executive may feel that he cannot fulfil his role as he would wish unless he attends political groups' meetings on a fairly regular basis. It may be that the political parties – both in power and in opposition – feel that such attendance is part of the job. The chief executive may

be responding to a desire from councillors which it would be short-sighted not to meet.

Where the chief executive does attend as matter of practice those meetings to which he is invited, there are some questions to which answers are needed.

a How long should he stay in the meeting? On the whole it seems undesirable to stay on after giving information and answering questions. The chief executive is not a member of the group and must do what he can to stand apart and preserve his position as the neutral paid head of the administration.

b Should he be accompanied by other officers? Clearly on any meeting to consider the budget, the chief financial officer seems essential. There may be other similar cases. However if the chief executive can act on his own as the liaison officer between the majority party and the administration, it lessens the area of risk to which attendance must in some degree give rise.

c Should he regularly attend minority party group meetings? As a general rule, it is suggested that he should not. Attendance at meetings of the majority party is justified because it provides a machinery for informed decisions to be taken by that party. It is seen as the means of getting the facts fed into the decision-making process before it is too late. It is seen as part of the special relationship with the majority party. None of these reasons apply to attendance at meetings of the minority party. However occasional attendance, with the knowledge of the majority party, may well be permissible.

As has been said, this whole area is developing and what works in one place might be suicidal in another. There are risks inherent in attendance at party group meetings. The chief executive should be aware of this, and on his guard against getting himself into a false long term position by the desire to make short term progress.

PARTY MEETINGS

I was only once asked to attend a party group meeting of the majority party, the Conservatives. It was about the budget and the treasurer and I went along together: we left after nearly two hours when we had explained matters and answered questions. Only councillors were present, though I would not have been put out if the regional chairman had been present. In general I think only councillors should attend when officers are present. After all, councillors would be surprised if the chief executive were accompanied by someone say on the staff of the Institute of Local Government Studies. The Labour Party leader was told what was on foot and was offered (with Conservative approval) a similar briefing session. The offer was not taken up, so my experience was far too limited to give me any personal feeling for any potential difficulties.

Politics and ethics

The chief executive is an employee of the council. He owes a clear duty of loyalty to them. He is also likely to be a professional man. He owes a duty of loyalty to his professional code of behaviour. Normally there should be no conflict between these two loyalties. The council should not, for example, expect a doctor to break a confidence. They should not ask a solicitor to take action which would amount to professional misconduct. If the council were to expect such unprofessional action, the officer would have to explain why he could not comply. In the case of professions with a degree of statutory regulation, the officer's position will be stronger than those whose profession is governed entirely by the rules of a professional institute. A solicitor for example could not continue to act as a solicitor to the council if he were struck off the rolls. A town planner on the other hand who was removed from the register of the Royal Town Planning Institute for breach of their professional code of conduct could still act (at least in theory) as chief planner to the council. If one disregards this difference between some professions and others, the professional man must clearly exercise his functions in conformity with any code of professional behaviour to which he is required to subscribe.

The chief executive and other chief officers are also under a duty to observe the law. The council may not require that officers act illegally. As Lord Justice Scott said in a case in 1948 (Blackpool Corpn v Locker (1948) All E.R. p 98), 'I think it right, to emphasize in the clearest possible terms that solicitors, who act as officers of local authorities, and in that capacity swear affidavits of documents, owe a duty to the court, to the opposite party, and to their own profession, to take proper care in the making of such affidavits, and, as solicitors, they cannot be heard to say that they do not understand the nature of the obligation imposed in swearing such affidavits.'

Hopefully there will be few cases of illegal instructions being given, but in the present era of conflict between central and local government it would be sanguine to suppose there will be none. Officers should not needlessly take up an exposed position. A witness in a criminal case may say, 'I will not give evidence voluntarily, but if you obtain a subpeona I will be obliged to attend'. So the officer faced with an instruction not to do something where there is a legal obligation to do so, for example under a contract, mortgage or other document binding the council, may similarly say, 'I will pay you, if I can have the protection of a Court Order to that effect'. Each case would require consideration on its merits.

If the chief executive and others owe a loyalty to their employer, to their profession and to the law, do they also owe some duty to the public? If they do, may that be a higher duty, transcending the normal duty to the employer? The question is similar to the one as to whether civil servants owe a duty to Parliament transcending the normal duty to their minister.

Two codes of conduct of local government professions – those of the Libraries Association and the British Association of Social Workers – specifically state that the duty to the client may outweigh the duty to the employer. Some support for this viewpoint was given by a remark made by Lord Caldecote, then Lord Chief Justice, in an audit case in 1944. Speaking of the office of the town clerk, Lord Caldecote said 'The office of town clerk is an important part of the machinery of local government. He may be said to stand between the borough council and the ratepayers. He is there to assist by his advice and action the conduct of public affairs in the borough'. The audit case itself was an illustration of the principle dealt with earlier in this chapter, that the town clerk owed a duty to the whole council to disclose important information. He was guilty of negligence and misconduct in not doing so. However, if Lord Caldecote was giving judicial approval to the view that the town clerk or chief executive could go over the heads of his council to the public, his remarks must be read in the light of the Report of Mr Ramsay Willis Q.C. (later Mr Justice Willis) on the Bognor Regis Inquiry in 1965. (An extract from this Report·and extracts from the judgements in the audit case form Appendix 6.3.

The Report doubted the correctness of Lord Caldecote's view. It did not rule out the possibility that in some quite exceptional circumstances some higher duty might arise. But it was unequivocal that the correct rule to be applied was that the town clerk owed his duty to the council who employed him:

'He is the employee of his Council and it is to them that his primary loyalty and duty lie and it is to them he is answerable for his actions'. Paragraphs 235–239 of the Report in the Appendix should be read in full because they provide admirable guidance to the chief executive in difficult situations. In all normal circumstances the chief executive is to do the job in the way the council want it done. This does not mean that the chief executive is to be a mere cypher or that he should keep silent on issues of policy. Mr Justice Cassels in the Finsbury case commented 'I find it difficult to picture a completely gagged town clerk'. It is one thing to be gagged. It is another thing to be over-eager to speak up. When the chief executive decides that there are views to be put forward, he should do so in a way which will cause the least embarrassment to the council's leadership. Normally this means giving advice in confidence. The timing of that advice can often be crucial. It should not be given at a time which may result in cutting the ground from under the feet of the majority party, e.g. weaken their position in negotiations with the Government. The position in such circumstances is not very different from that which has conventionally obtained where a council proposes to embark upon litigation. Advice about the likely success or failure of the law suit will not be made public for fear of giving comfort to the defendant or imperilling the prospects of a negotiated settlement. It is difficult to visualize the circumstances in which the chief executive might have to do more than inform the council as a whole and go over their heads to the public at large. Such action would not be justified by a conviction that services would suffer or that sections of the community might be at risk or that the council might be in breach of its statutory duty. These are views to put before the council, not the public, for it is the council who bear responsibility to the electorate, not the officers. It is in truth more than difficult to envisage a circumstance in which the chief executive would be justified in making an appeal to the ratepayers.

The price which the local government officer pays for his job security, whatever political changes may take place at elections, is the need to take action and implement policies which he may, personally or professionally, feel to be wrong or misguided. It is an essential part of the concept of the non-political, impartial officer serving the councils of this country that a senior officer cannot have the luxury of airing hostile views in public or criticizing his council's policies or actions. Those who want to do so, bring into question the validity of the concept of the impartial employee who can serve all masters. Senior council officers cannot have the best of both worlds – the freedom of a private citizen to criticize, and a public office which continues irrespective of political change. Those who cannot stand the heat of the kitchen should not take up cooking as a career.

The hung council

The growth of a third political force, the SDP-Liberal Alliance, has brought a new phenomenon to British local government, that of the hung council. There was occasionally a hung council in days gone by, in which no one party could command a majority. Such a council was then a rarity; now there are many.

The way in which the hung council will be run will vary from place to place and from time to time. There may be a formal coalition between two parties who together can command a majority in the council chamber. Or there may be an arrangement by which the smallest party holding the balance of power may allow the largest single party to assume control. In the latter case there will be no formal coalition, rather a policy of tacit agreement. Both types of arrangement have in-built tensions which are most likely to surface at the time of formulating the budget. The coalition may be unable to agree upon a budget. The majority party hitherto allowed to govern may find support withdrawn by the party holding the balance of power. And there are other circumstances which can upset the existing arrangements, bringing about new political alignments and with them a change in the current control of the council.

In the life of one council there may be several arrangements for political control. Today's Leader of the Council may be tomorrow's Leader of the Opposition.

Neither parties nor members can be labelled Majority, Opposition or Cross-bench, and the straightforward arrangements possible in a council with a clearly defined majority will require adjustment.

The chief executive in these circumstances is clearly operating against a background of political uncertainty, delay and often confusion. His role becomes crucially important. He can do much to maintain some degree of consistency of policy. He can make hastily constructed political arrangements more workable. He may become the custodian of commonsense in the political process.

With a hung council, the chief executive is manifestly the servant of the whole council. There is no need to put any gloss on this or to write in the need for a special relationship with the majority party. All the parties may be at one time or another part of the majority. So the chief executive must know and be on good terms with the leaders of all of them. His relationship with the Leader of the Council for the time being should not in principle be different in a hung council than in one with a majority party, i.e. close and frequent contact on the business of the council. The political context is clearly different, but the characteristics of the relationship are the same. It is in the relationships with the other parties that the picture changes. The chief executive needs to know what their policies are, what stance they are likely to adopt on major issues, what might be capable of compromise and what is immutable. The chief executive needs to create confidence with all the parties that he understands their objectives and can be relied upon, if the time comes, to assist them.

All this is not an easy task. It demands much hard work. The chief executive may find himself spending time talking with councillors which he feels could better be spent on straightforward management.

However, if the chief executive is not in a position to 'manage' the political processes, the council may fail to take sensible decisions at the right time. If the chief executive is well informed on all the major issues confronting the council and the attitudes which the different parties are likely to take to them, he is in a unique position to give advice formally and informally and to respond to approaches made to him.

Nowhere is his skill and patience more certain to be tested than over the budget. All parties will want information, briefing and discussion. The results of their various deliberations are unlikely to be known until the last minute. At the council meeting, a stalemate may develop which only the administration, led by the chief executive can resolve. Only he has a perception of what each party is trying to achieve. By acting as an interface between the parties, the chief executive may enable a sensible budget to be agreed by a majority.

In a hung council all parties need information and advice, whether through the conventional committee system or more informal channels. The chief executive must ensure that information is given accurately comprehensively and even-handedly; and that advice is given impartially, and where necessary, in confidence. He must ensure that chief officers do the same in relation to their committee chairmen and party spokesmen on those committees. Cheshire County Council have found it helpful to get the formal agreement of the political parties to the ground rules which should govern the rights of the parties to information and advice. The agreed conventions are set out in Appendix 6.2. It is instructive to compare this with the very much simpler concepts introduced in Cheshire when the Conservatives had a large majority (see Appendix 6.1). If conventions can be agreed, the chief executive becomes the custodian of the rules and the arbiter at first instance of their interpretation. This reinforces his role as the servant of the whole council, which becomes quite unambiguous in a hung council. Whether or not a particular council adopts written conventions, there is a clear need to get agreement between the parties covering such areas as entitlement to information; right to briefing; membership of informal working parties or panels of members; and the right to the use of various council services and departments.

Some hung councils may achieve a measure of political stability throughout the life of the council. In others, there may be several changes in the political alignments, so that control passes from one party to another. Even with some stability, the policies adopted by the council are likely to be an uneasy amalgam of the policies of two parties. In the worst case, there may be no policy at all, merely a succession of short-term expedients. The chief executive and chief officers, in regular contact with the party leaderships, may have a reasonable perception of what the council is trying to achieve at any given time and the reason for it. It is much more difficult for staff at say third, fourth or fifth tier to understand the position. They may merely detect delay and confusion, and be unsettled by the lack of traditional and familiar certainty. The chief executive should recognize this. He needs to arrange for regular briefing of all senior staff, who should be charged with the task of passing the message down the line. This should present no problem to those who have some regular system of briefing staff. For those who have none, special efforts must be made. A hung council can be a frustrating experience for everyone concerned, from the political leadership downwards. Whilst the top staff levels have the unusual challenge of making things work in conditions of political stalemate, those lower down may simply be upset and demotivated. If they feel that they are kept in the dark; if they have to rely on the local newspaper to tell them what is going on; if all they perceive is uncertainty, then demoralization of staff may set in. One of the prime tasks of the chief executive in a hung council is to see that this does not occur. The first step is to ensure that he shares his knowledge of the political scene with those who will have to try and implement the decisions reached by the council – and understand why those decisions have been reached in the way they have.

The hung council will test to the full the sensitivity and ability of the chief executive. He needs above everything else to gain the confidence of all the parties – no easy task for some party leaders are suspicious of the top paid staff. He will receive confidences and must respect them. He must not give in because simple things take inordinately long to achieve. He must carry his staff at all levels with him. He must recognize that a learning process is going on, not just for the administration but for the political parties themselves. In some councils there is no sign of a return effectively to a two-party system. It may be a long learning process, extending over the life of several councils.

If the emergence of substantial numbers of hung councils does one good thing it is to reinforce the British concept of a non-partisan, impartial paid administration. A chief executive or chief officer who was politically committed (and there are a few) would find it difficult to survive, let alone be effective, if he served a hung council.

Conclusion

Finally, there is the need to acknowledge the fact that there are a few councils where the reasoned and reasonable approach advocated in this chapter will make little headway. These cowboys of the political world want to ride roughshod over the minority councillors and the paid administrators alike. They may hold all the chairmanships, have one-party committees, amend Standing Orders to prevent questions and limit discussions, appoint their own political advisers and instruct the chief executive as to the stance he is to adopt on all the matters discussed earlier. They may resent advice and seek to appoint staff at senior level who share their views. There is not much guidance any text book can provide in these sort of circumstances. The chief executive must work out his own salvation. He may reflect on the fact that the British tradition of a professional, highly competent but politically neutral civil and local government service is one of the most admired features of our governmental system throughout the free world. He may draw comfort and inspiration from the fact that the office of town clerk is referred to in St Paul's Acts of the Apostles and that his own office springs from a long and honourable lineage in this country. The legal protection the office once enjoyed has been abolished, making independence of thought and action more personally hazardous than it should be. Yet the need for honest and impartial advice and for personal and professional integrity were never greater. When the going gets rough (as it can do even in the most courteously run councils) the chief executive should not flinch from doing what he believes to be right.

Appendix 6.1

CHESHIRE COUNTY COUNCIL: AGREED PROTOCOL GOVERNING THE POSITION OF THE PRINCIPAL MINORITY PARTY, DECEMBER 1974

Foreword

The guidelines in the appendix have been prepared for the use of chairmen of committees and chief officers. They are intended to give guidance as to the safeguarding of the interests of the principal minorty party, particularly where that party holds no chairmanships or vice-chairmanships.

The term 'minority representative' is used to indicate that member of the minority party who has been notified as being their spokesman or principal member on a particular committee or subject previously referred to as a 'shadow chairman'.

It will be for chief officers to remind chairmen as necessary of the appropriate guideline governing a particular case.

If there is any doubt as to the interpretation of these guidelines in any particular case, the chief officer will inform the chief executive who will refer the matter to the leaders of the majority and minority parties.

Relations with chief officers

a Should a chief officer require to inform a chairman of an important confidential matter, the chairman should normally authorize the chief officer similarly to inform the minority representative.

b If information of a general character is being provided to the chairman on the chief officer's initiative, the chairman should normally authorize the chief officer to provide a copy of the minority representative.

c If a chairman has asked for a brief from the chief officer to support a particular line being taken by the majority party, it would not be necessary or usual for the chairman to provide a copy to the minority representative.

d If information is given to any other member, the chairman must be sent a copy.

Conferences etc

a If county council representation at a conference, meeting or deputation is to extend beyond the chairman, accompanied by an officer or officers, the chairman should ask the committee to consider sending the vice- chairman (or other majority party member) and a representative of the principal minority party. Bearing in mind the need for economy, it should not be automatic that representation will extend beyond the chairman.

b If delegates are sent abroad, or to a government department to meet the minister, consideration should be given by the appropriate committee to sending three members i.e. chairman, vice-chairman and one other member being a representative of the principal minority party – the committee being again mindful of the need for economy.

c Where the chairman of the County Council is offering hospitality on a fairly wide scale, he should ensure that all parties are represented and for that purpose may consult the leader of the minority group. In the case of small special functions, the chairman will formulate his own list of guests having regard to the character and purpose of the function.

Agenda pre-meeting

It is for the chairman of each committee to decide which member or members should attend any briefing meeting e.g. vice-chairman or chairmen of sub-committees. It will not be obligatory upon the chairman to invite the principal minority representative to attend.

Support services

If support services are provided for any chairman of a committee, they need not also be provided for the minority representative on that committee. When accommodation and other factors allow for a more general provision of support services, consideration will be given to making arrangements for the minority groups.

Press statements

When a routine press statement is released by the Information Office a copy will be sent immediately to the appropriate chairman, but not to the minority representative.

When a chairman is consulted as to the contents of an important press statement, he may at his discretion ask for the minority representative to be consulted.

Appendix 6.2

CONVENTIONS ON RELATIONS BETWEEN THE POLITI CAL PARTIES REPRESENTED ON THE COUNCIL, FEBRUARY 1983 (ABRIDGED)

Entitlement to information

Any member of the council may ask the appropriate chief officer for written factual information about a department or service. Such requests will be met subject to any legal requirements and the following para. A copy of the chief officer's response will be given to the chairman of the appropriate committee, unless the information provided is of a routine or minor nature.

If a chief officer considers that information requested could only be provided at unreasonable cost he shall seek direction from the chairman of the committee as to whether it should be provided.

Where a chairman or vice-chairman asks a chief officer for information, that information will not normally be supplied to the spokesmen of other parties.

Where a chief officer on his own initiative provides information to a committee chairman, that information will be supplied to the spokesmen of other parties, unless it is of a routine or minor nature, subject to the approval of the chairman.

Briefings on committee business

Formal briefings will be arranged for the chairman and vice-chairman (jointly) of committees to consider the business to be transacted at each meeting as set out on the agenda. The chairman may at his or her discretion invite other appropriate chairmen or vice-chairmen, or spokesmen of other parties, to attend such briefings.

Any party not holding the chair or vice-chair of a commitee may request a briefing on the business to be transacted at a committee meeting. Such a request shall be made by the leader or relevant spokesman to the chief executive who will make the appropriate arrangements with the chief officer(s) concerned. The chairman of the committee concerned shall be informed that such a briefing has been given.

Briefing of party groups

In addition to the formal arrangements described above, all parties may request a private and confidential briefing, including, but where appropriate going beyond, the provision of written information, on matters of policy which are or may become the subject of discussion by the council or any committee.

Such a request shall be made by the leader or relevant spokesman of the party concerned to the chief executive who will make the appropriate arrangements with the chief officer(s) concerned. A chief officer may nominate a member of his staff to provide such a briefing.

Panels established by committees

Subject to standing orders a committee may establish a panel of members to consider an issue in more detail on an ad hoc or standing basis, with or without delegated decision-making powers.

Places on such panels shall be allocated to the political parties on the same basis as are places on committees i.e. in the proportions in which the parties are represented on the council with appropriate rounding to whole numbers. Places on panels for co-opted members of committees are excluded from this arrangement.

The chairman of such panels shall be the chairman of the parent committee and the membership shall where appropriate include the vice-chairman and party spokesmen.

Dates of committee and panel meetings

Subject to the duty of Selection Sub-Committee to prepare the calendar of meetings of committees, where a chairman of a committee or panel wishes to call a meeting or vary a date of a meeting he or she shall first arrange for the spokesmen of the other parties to be consulted.

Appointment of representatives

The appointment of representatives to any outside body of a permanent nature or involving regular attendance will be made by the Selection Sub-Committee, confirmed when time permits by the Parliamentary and Organization Committee. That sub-committee will also determine questions relating to approved duty.

Where an invitation to the Council to be represented at a conference or other occasion is confined to one member, the committee in question should normally be recommended to apoint the chairman or his or her nominee.

Where the invitation is to appoint more than one representative, and the occasion in the opinion of the committee so justifies, consideration should be given to appointing in addition the vice-chairman and/or the spokesmen of other parties as necessary in order to achieve an appropriate political balance.

Services for Members and Party Groups

Accommodation will be provided for members on a basis to be determined by the Parliamentary and Organization Committee, after consultation with the party leaders.
Clerical and typing services will be made available to the Chairman and Leader of the Council.

Any request for similar services for other members will be referred to the Parliamentary and Organization Committee after consultation with the party leaders.

Reprographic services will be provided for the use of party groups by the County Secretariat subject to the availability of resources, at a cost to be determined from time to time by the Parliamentary and Organization Committee.

Press statements and relations with the media

Official press statements will be issued on behalf of the County Council or a committee by the Public Relations and Information Officer. They will be made with the agreement of the chairman of the council/committee as relevant, subject to any appropriate consultation with party leaders or spokesmen.

Press statements arising out of council business issued in a party capacity by the leader or spokesman of any party may at his request be processed by the public relations and information officer; any costs incurred will be charged to the party issuing the statement. Chief Officers may be requested to provide factual information to assist in the preparation of such statements.

Chief Officers may deal with any request for information or questions asked by the press, television or radio, and may accept invitations to broadcast or appear on television in order to give the facts of a situation or explain the council's policies. Where possible the appropriate chairman should be informed as soon as practicable.

Review

These conventions will be reviewed annually.

The chief executive will initiate a special review at any time if required by a change in the political balance on the council or in the appointments of committee chairmen, or on the request of any of the parties.

Appendix 6.3

Extract from the Report of Mr Ramsay Willis QC to the Minister for Housing and Local Government and the Chairman of the Bognor Regis Urban District Council on the Bognor Regis Inquiry, 1965.

Chapter 29 – the root of the difficulties

229 I do not think it is possible to come to any conclusion on the events which took place in Bognor between July 1964 and May 1965, without considering the personalities of those involved. I have attempted, therefore, when considering each of the principal actions and events during the time when Mr Smith was clerk of the council, to arrive at an understanding of the motives of those concerned. As a result, I have come to the conclusion that at the root of the difficulties which arose between Bognor Regis Council and their clerk lay, first, a fundamental difference in their conception of their own and each others roles in local government, and second, the personality of Mr Smith.

230 The next chapter of this part of the report contains my views on the difference in the way the council and the clerk saw their respective roles. In the three chapters following that are my comments, in the light of the two factors which I believe to have been fundamental to the difficulties which arose, on some of the principal events described in Part I of the report.

Chapter 30 – the conflict of view

231 Mr Smith considers that the clerk of a council, if he is a lawyer, should act as the council's legal adviser; in so doing he is advising the council in his speciality just as the engineer advises on engineering matters, and all the other chief officers provide the council with the benefit of their professional and technical knowledge. But the clerk is also the chief administrative officer of the council, unless it is specifically stated to the contrary, and as such the clerk is 'first among equals' in his relationship with the council's other chief officers.

232 With this view of the office of clerk, the Bognor Regis Council, the Society of Clerks of Urban District Councils and nearly everyone in the world of local government would, I think, agree with Mr Smith.

233 Mr Smith, however, goes further, and believes that the clerk of a council bears a unique responsibility among chief officers in that he enjoys a very special relationship with the ratepayers. He finds support for this view, as he has said on a number of occasions, in the judgement given by Lord Chief Justice Caldecote in the case of Hurle-Hobbs ex. p. Riley, 1944, known as the 'Finsbury Case', which is concerned with district audit. The section of the judgement which Mr Smith considers to be relevant appears in his letter of 25th May to all councillors (see Chapter 28(b)) and is as follows:

'The office of town clerk is an important part of the machinery of local government. He may be said to stand between the borough council and the ratepayers. He is there to assist by his advice and action the conduct of public affairs in the borough, and if there is a disposition on the part of the council, still more on the part of any member of the council, to ride roughshod over his opinions, the question must at once arise as to whether it is not his duty forthwith to resign his office or at any rate, to do what he thinks right and await the consequences. This is not so dangerous or heroic a course as it may seem. The integrity of the administration of public affairs is such that publicity may be safely relied upon to secure protection for anyone in the position in which the town clerk was said to have been placed.'

234 The observations of the Lord Chief Justice were made in the context of the facts of the Finsbury Case and seem to me not to have been necessary to his decision on that case. Whether I am right or not, I think it is clear that Lord Caldecote was not intending to lay down a principle of local government practice of universal application and irrespective of the circumstances.

235 The acceptance of the passage quoted above as definitive of the clerk's duties in all circumstances and at all times would place him in a unique position indeed. It would seem to follow from the acceptance of that view that in any situation in which a clerk found himself in conflict with his council over an important issue of policy, he would have a duty, if it was his opinion that the wishes of the council were opposed to the best interests of the ratepayers, 'to do what he thinks right'; indeed, the clerk might conceive it to be his duty to make every effort to frustrate the will of his council and to appeal, over their heads, for the support of the ratepayers. If a clerk were to interpret the words of Lord Caldecote in the way suggested above, it is clear the he could consider that his first duty was to the ratepayers and that he was virtually independent of his council.

236 But if a clerk is not answerable to his council he is answerable to no one. In my view he is the employee of his council and it is to them that his primary loyalty and duty lie and it is to them that he is answerable for his actions. In the course of advising his council there is clearly no objection to a clerk telling them that he considers their proposals to be wrong and, if he thinks fit, submitting his views to them in writing. I consider, however, that he should express his opinion in a manner that will not embarrass his council and that once his view is known to them he should leave them to come to their own decision. It is the duty of councillors to formulate the policy for the local authority and they are directly answerable for their actions to the ratepayers at the polls. This was the view of their own and their clerk's function that was held by the Bognor Regis Council, as I think, correctly.

237 In exceptional circumstances, such as those in the Finsbury Case, there could well be a justification for a clerk departing from what I have suggested should be his normal behaviour vis-à-vis councillors. If he believes that a member of the council had either consciously or unconsciously committed, or is putting himself in a position in which he might commit, an offence then I think he should first broach the matter with the councillor himself; if that fails he should inform the Chairman of the Council of his concern and, perhaps, consult the Leader on the Council of the Party to which the councillor in question belongs. If after all these efforts the clerk finds that no notice has been taken of his warning, naturally, he finds himself in a difficult situation. If he is satisfied that there is a prima facie case of, for example, an offence under section 76 of the Local Government Act, 1933, after making efforts to alert the Chairman and Councillor concerned, I think he would be justified in confiding his suspicions to the Director of Public Prosecutions.

238 However, it seems to me that it would be quite improper if the clerk were to do anything which might create the impression in the minds of the public or the press that he was suspicious of his council or any member of it. It is perhaps otiose to add that a man is innocent until the courts have found him guilty, but the public seems all too ready to believe that the mere suggestion of impropriety is sufficient proof of guilt.

239 I have heard evidence from the Society of Clerks of Urban District Councils and from people who have served for many years in local government either as councillors or officers. I am satisfied that none of them share the view – quoted by Mr Smith on several occasions – that the Clerk 'may be said to stand between the Borough Council and the ratepayers'.

AUTHOR'S ADDITION

Mr Ramsay Willis only quoted part of Viscount Caldecote's judgement on the Town Clerk and it seems worth including this preamble which preceded the quotation in the Report. It also seems appropriate to include what Mr Justice Cassels said, bearing in mind that the case is unreported except in Hurle-Hobbs Law relating to District Audit.

THE LORD CHIEF JUSTICE, VISCOUNT CALDECOTE

'I can deal more shortly with the case as it concerns the town clerk. Mr Turner did not dispute that the town clerk had a duty to disclose information which was in fact kept back, but he submitted that being subordinate to Alderman Riley, he was not guilty of misconduct. Imprudence there may have been, but imprudence is not misconduct. Notwithstanding the strenuous contention of counsel on his behalf, the town clerk seems to me wholly to misconceive his duty when he says that although he thought that the matters I have discussed ought to have been disclosed to the council, he was entitled to stand by without taking such steps as were open to him merely because he would otherwise have been liable to dismissal from his office without notice. It was a little surprising to me that such an argument should be advanced on his behalf. It seems to me to be tantamount to an admission of misconduct. It suggests that the town clerk put his private interests above his duty in his office.'

MR JUSTICE CASSELS

'Mr Turner, on behalf of the Appellant Mr James, the town clerk, urged that he was merely a servant, that he was subject to dismissal at the pleasure of the council, that he had no security of tenure, that Alderman Riley threatened him with dismissal if he disclosed what Alderman Riley did not wish to be disclosed, that neither the finance agreement nor the deep shelter was *ultra vires*, that the reason there was no benefit was that the war broke out too soon, and that it was Alderman Riley who found the man to bring the friendly action. Not one of these submissions provides any excuse for the town clerk, occupying the position he did, failing to bring to the notice of the council what was happening, failing to explain the very burdensome agreement into which they were entering, failing to say anthing to the Law and Parliamentary Committee about the action, and failing to produce the adverse report. It was said that the town clerk could not address the council. I find it difficult to picture a completely gagged town clerk. These were important matters essential for the consideration of the council. In being a party to what happened, the town clerk was guilty of negligence and misconduct.'

7 Square pegs in square holes

'Thou art not for the fashion of these times
Where none will sweat but for promotion.'

Shakespeare – As You Like It

The personnel function

Personnel work has been one of the big growth areas since the reorganization of 1974. It is an established specialist sphere which continues to increase in importance, as manpower and industrial relations dominate much of policy making.

However high ranking the personnel director, the chief executive must regard himself (and others must regard him) as *the* personnel director. Something between 60% and 70% of a local authority's budget is spent on salaries and wages. Local government is labour intensive. It always has been so and it is difficult to see the new technology making more than a marginal difference to this historic position. The recruitment, training, development, motivation and reward of staff must therefore be a matter of major concern. No one will wish to neglect the possibility of improving performance and input by installing new technology. No one wishes to condemn staff to work with out of date, unreliable or wasteful plant, appliances, or machinery whether on site or in the office. Yet the fact remains that the main expectation of better value for money across the whole range of local government services must lie in improving individual performance. The chief executive can make a major contribution by the stance he adopts; by his example; and by the policies he seeks to introduce. There must be many things he will leave to his personnel director. But the main thrust of policy for manpower should come from the top.

In the entrepreneurial world outside local government, the importance of individual performance is fully recognized. If profits are not being made, if work is in arrears, if budgets are overspent, the search is for the individual responsible. The question is, why is he not performing? Action will then be taken to motivate, warn and support and if that fails, to replace or remove. More drastic action can be undertaken than would be acceptable in present-day local government because everyone accepts that the survival of the firm depends upon its success. The organization is seen to be no stronger than its weakest links and the livelihood of all can be seen to be imperilled if poor performers are not moved to areas more suitable to their abilities – or even moved out. Provided such action is seen to be fair and necessary, it can be taken in a way that would be difficult or impossible in a local authority. The history and tradition of local government – indeed the public service generally – is so different, that the importance of personal performance seems to have become obscured. When things are not going right, new hierarchical structures are devized or changes in organization are made. Working parties are set up or in–depth studies put in hand. Poor structure of an organization can certainly inhibit performance, but the tendency to look at structure first is to have unrealistic priorities. It is the people who matter, and it is why they are not performing that is the real question, a question often evaded because it is more difficult in the public service to reward exceptional performance or to penalize that which is bad. Hence the enthusiasm for new organization charts, working practice directives or other remedies which do not overtly admit that Mr X is not capable of doing his job. The object of the new structure may of course be to put Mr X in a new position where he can do no harm. But the whole approach blurs the importance of individual responsibility and individual competence.

When it was difficult to get staff in the late 1960s and early 1970s, the complaints were that departments were 'not up to establishment'. Only rarely were complaints made about the quality of the available intake, or was it suggested that there might be fewer but better quality and better paid appointments. Numbers, establishments, structures, organization charts have dominated local government thinking for too long.

Recruitment

When it is so difficult to dismiss or demote incompetent staff, it is astonishing that local government procedures for making appointments are for the most part perfunctory in the extreme. This may reflect once again this preoccupation with posts and establishments rather than performance of the individual. It is probably also a legacy of the overheated economy of the 1960s and 1970s when there were acute shortages of many varieties of skilled or even unskilled staff. To have well thought-out processes of selection may seem a needless luxury if there are only one or two applicants for a vacancy. That situation no longer obtains and the casual approach of past decades has no justification today. The main selection technique in local government is the interview. Yet those interviewing are but rarely given any course of instruction of the sort adopted for example by the police or civil service who teach interviewing on a regular and continuous basis. Little or no use is made of tests, group selection or psychological assessment.

RECOGNIZING YOUR LIMITATIONS

When John Tyzack was partly retired he came to Cheshire to talk to a seminar on selection run for chairmen of committees and senior officers. He was one of the early gurus in the business of professional selection. As we sat in the back of the county Rolls on the way from the station he said two things which I remember. The first was that he still believed that careful interviewing was the best selection tool for senior posts. He did not decry aptitude tests or psychological tests, but his faith was in the unhurried interview by a trained interviewer. The second was that he was no longer prepared to interview anyone under 35. 'Their dress, their attitudes, their beards – lots of things – put me off. I don't relate to them well. At 65, I think the age gap is too great for me to do a good job'. My own experience in interviewing young graduates who wished to be articled to me led me to a broadly similar conclusion. They all looked the same. I did not think I made a great success of interviewing them. From thenceforth I left their selection to others younger than I was.

The chief executive is preeminently the man who can ensure that the recruitment policies of his authority match the best that is available elsewhere. His first task must be to secure that councillors are only involved in those appointments which are truly theirs – chief officers and deputies, and other posts where the post-holder must relate frequently to some group of elected members so that his or her acceptability to them may be regarded as a major factor. Chief officers in charge of departments must feel fully accountable for the success of the department. This accountability will be diminished if staff appointments are made at many levels by councillors. Some chief officers may even welcome a situation where accountability is fudged. If things go wrong it may be possible to say: 'We could do no better with the staff *you* gave us.' The policy of restricting councillor involvement to the top appointments only, is not put forward in any 'hands-off-my-affairs' spirit but basically to strengthen the accountability and the feeling of accountability of the paid administration for the success of that administration. There are other reasons for restricting the councillors' role besides the councillors' lack of managerial responsibility. The councillor may or may not have any skill at selection. And he rarely sees how those he appoints at levels below the top actually perform in the job, so he is deprived of any yardstick by which to measure the success or failure of past selection decisions. Some compromises will nevertheless have to be reached on the pure doctrine just enunciated. Working relationships with a chairman of a committee may require that he or she is involved in some way in some staff appointments. The area of involvement should be kept as small as is necessary not to disturb harmonious working. The chief officer should not use the factor of member involvement as an excuse for avoiding making a decision on an appointment which should be in the last resort his alone to make.

1001 APPLICATIONS

Whilst many posts in the 1960s and 1970s attracted few applicants, Cheshire's advertisement for a countryside officer (the first in any Authority) drew over 1000 applications. This imposed a considerable strain on the administrative machine, but even more so raised the question how to produce a short list. We decided to apply some fairly simple rules designed to reduce the number to more manageable proportions. First anyone over age 50 would be deleted, unless his present salary was over £x   (a few retiring service personnel came within this exception). Secondly anyone not currently earning a specified salary figure would be deleted unless he held a degree in estate management (or similar) or offered relevant experience in leisure activities. Very many applications were caught in the mesh of two tests, so that finally I was presented with about 100 applications, of which I selected about 25 for preliminary interview. The successful candidate Major Peter Moore was a serving officer in the Royal Engineers with NATO in Denmark.

Probably nothing gives the flavour of that overheated economy, the period when candidates interviewed you, than this letter received at the time.

I enclose an acknowledgement which was mysteriously sent to me by your department after I had applied for the post of ARTICLED CLERK, following the invitation by personal letter of the Clerk of the County Council. Whilst I have no doubt that the appointment of COUNTRYSIDE OFFICER is likely to lead to rewarding and satisfying work, I feel that I really ought to exploit further the fact that I will be graduating in June with a degree in Law. I abandoned Nature Study at the age of ten, and feel unqualified to supervise happenings in your delicious Cheshire countryside.

If the mistake has arisen through any stupidity on my part, which is unlikely, I would like to withdraw any purported application for the post of Countryside Officer; further, I have no desire to be a rat-catcher, a sewer inspector, or a gamekeeper: in spite of D. H. Lawrence, I feel my talents lie elsewhere. If possible at this late date, I would still be happy to be considered for the post for which I orginally applied, provided such a request does not throw too great a strain on the administrative and intellectual resources of your staff.

Yours in puzzlement,

If the chief executive can get agreement with councillors on their respective spheres of responsibility, his next task must be to get the agreement of departmental heads as to the role which the central personnel function should have within the organization. His ability to act here may be circumscribed by the historical development of the function within the authority. On the whole, local authorities seem to have opted, sensibly, for small central personnel departments or sections, leaving departments to run their own affairs within guidelines on important issues, prepared at the centre. A very large authority may have to centralize personnel work, but the advantages of moving in this direction must be balanced against the loss of departmental accountability which needs strengthening wherever possible. The areas in recruitment which might be covered by central directives include the following:

1 A standard job application form, capable of departmental additions or amendment where necessary.

2 A policy on external advertisement – always an expensive item and needing control in some form.

3 The numbers and composition of interviewing panels. The chief executive should encourage the use of multi-disciplinary panels, so that planners are not appointed solely by planners, educationalists by educationalists and so forth.

4 Procedures for controlling internal promotion. In-breeding has been the scourge of some local authorities. The chief executive must have a point of control to ensure some degree of balance between internal and external appointments. Trade unions will be closely interested in this especially during an era of manpower recession.

5 A policy on starting salaries. This will probably include limited flexibility to departments, with reference to the centre only on starting salaries beyond the limits.

Besides knowing that good selection procedures are in force throughout the organization, the chief executive needs to decide which appointments he will be personally involved in. It goes without saying that he must be concerned with the selection of the principal chief officers. The chief executive may be the leader of the team, but his work as captain will depend not only on his leadership abilities but the strengths of the team members. When the opportunity occurs, the chief executive must try and strengthen his team. By careful personal enquiries and giving adequate time to the selection process, the risk of a poor choice can be much reduced. Because he is head of the paid administration, and responsible for it, he is entitled to ask councillors to respect his views about candidates for filling a vacancy among his chief officers.

Deputy chief officers are also of great importance to the organization. A deputy often succeeds his chief. The wise chief executive will find time to be involved in the appointment of deputy chief officers. Time spent in getting the right people is never wasted. A chief officer will usually welcome the interest of the chief executive, who brings to the making of the deputy's appointment a wider spectrum of knowledge of the general market than a departmental head is likely to have. The chief executive will not be there to ram his views on the candidates down the throat of the chief officer, but to give a more detached assessment of the strength and weaknesses of the contenders and to compare the candidates with others he has seen recently. This is particularly valuable where there are internal candidates seeking promotion.

Recruitment is an area in which the outside world can judge the style and efficiency of the authority. Failure to be told the result of the application; poor interviewing; difficulties over expenses; inability to get information – all these and more tell the applicant something about the authority. The applicant will tell others. If the chief executive has the reputation of his authority at heart, he will see that the whole process of recruitment is not only an exercise in efficiency but a test in public relations as well.

REFEREES

Written references have their value, but nothing is better than to talk on the 'phone to people who know the candidate. Provided that there is not too long a gap, it may pay to go back to the last but one employer. He will not be trying to unload the candidate on to you or have his freedom to speak inhibited by feelings of loyalty to someone he works with. I once learned from a penultimate employer that a candidate we were interested in was an alcoholic (the one thing John Tyzack said that you could rarely learn from an interview).

In looking at candidates I found it helpful to ask myself the question 'If this were my business and I had to make profits from it, am I reasonably sure that this candidate will add to profitability?' I do not see how anyone can be sure if their only knowledge is a formal committee interview, coupled with some written references. It is not easy to pick winners. Preliminary interviews (maybe occasionally more than one), backed by diligent enquiries will reduce the risk of the ultimate decision being a disaster. Ideally the final choice should be made from a long list narrowed down as a result of preliminary interviews to no more than three candidates. For preliminary interviews for a chief officer, I would usually be joined by the chairman of the committee, as well as the retiring chief. I also made much use of assessors. Professor John Stewart of INLOGOV, for example, acted in this way on the appointment of a chief executive to succeed me: Mr Christopher Jonas of the London firm of chartered surveyors, Drivers Jonas, assisted with the appointment of a new county valuer. And there were others.

Training

As a nation we place less importance on training in the job than many other European countries. For many people – and local government is no exception – training is a frill or luxury, the first thing to be squeezed out in hard times. The fact that the nation's most successful enterprises are those which give high priority to training, may not carry much weight with councillors.

It took the arrival of the American fast food chains to make British caterers see that they must employ similarly well-trained staff to survive. Many a training-oriented chief executive must wish that there was some similar competitive spur to training in the local government service, in itself traditionally a laggard within the public service. So the standards on which cut-backs may be made are in themselves low by comparison with many other public bodies. What can the chief executive do about this?

First he must understand why training is necessary. He must be convinced himself, if he is to convince others. He must recognize that however good the selection process, some square pegs will be chosen for round holes. There may be only limited freedom to change the shape of the job. However, with training the square post holder may be rounded, so that there is a tolerable fit. On-the-job training of this sort need not cost a great deal. It does however need managers who understand the importance of training their subordinates.

The most voiced single complaint of managers is 'lack of experienced staff'. Many of those who complain loudest seem least to recognize that experienced staff are trained staff – trained by someone about the job and how to do it.

If the chief executive believes in training, he will try and get this concept across, understood at all levels of management. He will counter the oft-heard argument 'It takes me longer to supervise Miss X than to do it myself'. Managers who take this view have de-motivated staff who feel underused and underemployed. There are more staff in local authorities who feel undervalued and underused than those who feel that the pressures are too great.

Besides on-the-job training there is a need for some elements of formal instruction. Subjects like chairmanship/speaking in public; letter and report writing; clerical procedures; secretarial skills and many others are best dealt with by formal courses. A large authority can mount these for itself, specially tailored to its own needs and philosophies. Where it does so, the chief executive can demonstrate his involvement in training by giving occasionally the opening or closing talk at some programme in which he has a special interest. Where equipment exists, a videotaped message or address can be provided. Though this has obviously less impact than a personal appearance, it is a valuable means of involvement which makes less demand on time. The chief executive of a smaller authority may have to use courses run by others, whether inside local government, e.g. by other authorities or the provincial councils, or by private firms or nonprofit making bodies like the Industrial Society. Or he may be able to get several neighbouring authorities to join together to provide a course of training to meet a perceived need common to all of them.

The temptation to do nothing or to accept budget cuts without argument must be resisted. Training and development of staff is too important for the battle to be conceded merely because some shortsighted councillors find spending on training to be unpalatable in an era of recession.

Finally, the chief executive should not ignore his own training. Much of that will come from attending management development courses (a day or half a day) organized for his own top managers. It is stimulating and rewarding nevertheless to attend the occasional workshop or seminar, particularly on some new or less familiar subject. Courses and study days for senior executives run by such bodies as the British Institute of Management provide the added dimension of bringing the chief executive into contact with those in commerce and industry. Certainly once or twice a year, the chief executive should find the time to attend some events which will either add to his professional knowledge, enlarge his horizon or both. Ideally, he should plan his own training and have something like a development programme covering subjects about which he sees the need for fuller knowledge and information. A programme of this sort, however tentative, will prevent the selection on impulse of some seminar merely because the time, place or fee is right.

8 Involving the staff – and the members

Like people in many other organizations, local government staff are prepared to work in their own little cell, incurious about what is going on in the organization as a whole. There are often strong departmental loyalties, but even within a department there may be a degree of monastic seclusion so that, for example, payroll staff have little concept of internal audit, or the legal conveyancers of the work of the committee sections, or the students' grant staff of the primary eduction section. Staff are content not to know. Their interest is limited by the extent of their personal contacts. Their desire for knowledge is limited to information on those things which directly affect them – changes in working practices, holiday arrangements, salary increases and the like.

The chief executive in handling the internal relations of the authority should have two main objectives:

1 promoting a sense of loyalty to the organization as a whole, in addition to loyalty to some part of it;

2 ensuring that all staff are regularly informed of the policies problems and achievements of the authority.

There is a considerable degree of interaction between these two objectives. A sense of corporate loyalty can hardly be achieved without some effort to inform. The provision of information can of itself help to promote the feeling of belonging to something bigger than a section or department.

Corporate loyalty

Many observers have pointed out that local government is heavily departmentalized. The position that existed in the days prior to the

1974 reorganization is succinctly summarized in the following quotation from the Report of the Committee on the Management of Local Government in 1967:

'There exists therefore in local authorities in this country an organization which is based on separate parts, in each of which there is gathered the individual service with its professional departmental hierarchy led by a principal officer and supervising it a committee of members. There may be unity in the parts, but there is disunity in the whole.'

The reasons for this departmentalization can be found in the historical development of local government. Education ceased to be autonomous under *ad hoc* boards in 1902 but in many councils remained very much a self-contained service for at least the next half century. The poor law function was transferred to county councils and county boroughs in 1938 but in some authorities ran as a virtually separate function until the passing of the National Assistance Act 1948. More recent changes such as the abolition of separate Childrens and Welfare Departments and their merger into the new Social Services Departments in 1970 contained within them the seeds of possible future disunity. Old loyalties die hard, and it can take many decades before there is commitment from everyone to the new order of things.

The chief executive needs knowledge of the broad sweep of development of local government in this century, if he is to understand the obstacles to promoting a sense of corporateness in all staff.

DE MINIMIS

My experience in trying to introduce a more corporate approach to the activities of the Cheshire County Council was that you met more opposition over the small than the large changes.

It was over trivia that one or other departmental head would dig his toes in and assert his independence – trivia such as a standard job application form: an agreed format for advertising or a standard form of internal memorandum. The classic example of asserting independence for its own sake was the chief officer who objected to the internal memo form because it began 'From' followed by 'To' with a space for the addressee to be typed in. The addressee should, he argued, be in the first line – 'To' – and the name of the department originating it – 'From' – should be underneath – the reverse of what all other departmental heads had agreed. There must be at least six good reasons in favour of either proposition and I have heard them all. In general I tried to accept that the corporate approach could be painful to those on the receiving end. If they wished to flex their muscles to assert their independence over some minor matter, I preferred to let them do so unless and until some suitable opportunity might arise to raise the matter. In the long run, most personal idiosyncracies will disappear as those who hold them move on. As a judge once said to me cynically 'Whilst there's death, there's hope'.

The reorganization of 1974 has in many areas made both more necessary and more difficult the creation of a corporate spirit. The merger of several councils to form a single new unit has clearly made it necessary to create a new image for each new authority. The fact that many are still working from several separate locations makes it more difficult to pull the whole operation together into unity.

The chief executive may be conscious of the reasons for separateness and convinced of the need for corporateness, but how is he to achieve it?

First he should understand that although this chapter treats 'internal' relations as something separate from 'external' or public relations (dealt with in Chapter 11), they are but two sides of a single coin.

The staff are part of the public. If the public are well informed, the staff will be. The information-giving process can be slanted towards staff, when an occasion presents itself. There is every reason from time to time to use the information-giving service to the public to help to build staff morale and a sense of belonging to a progressive and efficient unit of local government.

If a chief executive wants to promote a sense of corporate loyalty, he must do all he can to encourage and support departmental loyalty. A soldier is unlikely to feel pride in being in the army, if he has no sense of pride in serving in his regiment. Departmental study days, departmental news sheets, and departmental social events all help to promote departmental loyalty. They can also be used to project the concept of corporate loyalty. Time or space can be found to say something of the work of other departments with whom there are day to day contacts. The chief executive can seek an invitation to appear and take some part in a study day; or even a social event for example by putting up a small prize and presenting it. Fierce departmental loyalty is sometimes seen as a barrier to the development of corporate loyalty and a corporate approach. It can be so. But if there is no departmental loyalty there is not much hope of corporate loyalty. What is needed is to take the blinkers off and direct some part of the loyalty to the organization as a whole.

CHANGING ATTITUDES

To help weld together the department I inherited in 1964, I took the whole of the staff (including junior clerks) for two days to a residential training college. We had a varied programme, most of it participatory in nature, with little if any formal instruction. The value of this lay not just, or even mainly, in the discussions. It was in the fact of being together, away from the workplace, with the opportunity to talk informally in the evenings. The residential element in training is a great producer of esprit de corps and affords unrivalled opportunities to change attitudes.

The same sort of benefit was obtained when chief officers and deputies spent two days at IBM laboratores at Hursley to discuss the future of the Cheshire computer services. This seminar was repeated some years later to assess new technological developments, including the mini-computer. On both occasions the benefit was not confined to a better understanding of the new technology, and its implications for management. The benefits from training activities are not just in greater knowledge or technical know-how. Training can transform attitudes to work, to other departments, and to the role of the council in society.

The chief executive cannot promote a corporate image and a sense of corporate loyalty on his own. He needs the help of every chief officer. Corporate loyalty starts at the top. If there is commitment at the top, ways will be found to see that the concept of corporate loyalty, given time, can permeate through the whole organization. There are many good reasons for the chief executive to be fair and evenhanded in his dealings with departments. One of them is that if he is seen to favour one department, he begins to deny the concept of corporateness to which he pays lip service.

In dealing with mature staff with long years of service it can be an uphill task to change attitudes. Not so with those newly recruited. The chief executive should ensure that at least once a year all those who have joined the authority can take part in an induction course. This in itself will promote corporate loyalty with newcomers. Explaining the whole range of the authority's functions will give them the wider horizon which is desirable.

A major spin-off from staff training activities is the promotion of a feeling of belonging to the larger unit, because staff from different departments mix together in a classroom atmosphere and in discussion. This not only helps them to understand the approach of staff from other disciplines, but tends to break down departmental barriers. The gains are even greater if the course can be residential, because the time for social meetings is increased. It is often over the dinner table and at the bar that barriers begin to crumble.

One of the great producers of a separatist approach in staff is the fact that so many spend their whole careers in a single department. Departments can become very self-contained for promotion purposes. This can be very unfair to those working in small departments who may be condemned to waiting for dead men's shoes.

The chief executive must do what he can to promote movement from one department to another, particularly at administrative level where a specialist technical qualification is not required. Internal promotions should be subject to some form of check to make departmental inbreeding more difficult, and there needs to be an agreed policy designed to help movement across departmental boundaries. However, if there is no real agreement about the desirability of such a policy, the procedures will probably be used to unload failures from one department to another.

By secondments of higher level staff to work for limited periods outside their own departments, e.g. an educationalist working with the police on truancy; by joint working parties drawn widely and not just from those with a primary interest; by multi-department staff appointment panels and in many other ways, the chief executive must seek to promote a loyalty to the authority and a conviction that the authority is a good one to work for.

Corporate information

Staff, being members of the public, will enjoy whatever information is provided to the local community by means of the press, radio and television. Because there is sometimes abbreviation of press statements and releases, it is sensible to see that copies of the actual text are available to staff – on departmental notice boards or otherwise. The point has already been made that what is sent to the media can be slanted so as to have a spin off in terms of staff relations.

Yet clearly no authority should rely only on its general information giving machinery to provide staff with the knowledge they need. The chief executive should be prepared to use every channel to get across to staff not only those matters which directly concern them, but also the wider perspective of the authority's problems and successes which marks out the difference between the pedestrian and the pace-setting authority. How this is done will vary from one authority to another, because size, dispersion of staff, tradition, and availability of resources (both manpower and money) will affect the answers.

Appendix 8.1 provides a check list of different ways of getting information across, from simple means to the sophisticated, all of which have been used successfully by different authorities.

Whatever other means are adopted for communicating with staff, the chief executive should seek opportunities of speaking himself to gatherings of staff about matters of current importance. This involves a considerable effort. Suitable locations have to be found and reserved. Times chosen must maximize the probability of a good attendance. Staff must be informed far enough in advance. And the chief executive must give the time needed not only to attend, but to prepare a script which says something worth hearing. Carried out sparingly, face to face gatherings of this sort can be very rewarding. Staff in remote locations feel that they are not forgotten. The chief executive will learn a great deal from the reactions of his different audiences.

HOLDING THE STAGE

When Cheshire was threatened with abolition in the Report of the Royal Commission, I decided that I would speak to as many staff as I could to say what the council were doing to oppose the plan. This included besides a public relations campaign, the engagement of P.A. Management Consultants to estimate the cost of implementing the proposals of the Royal Commission. My first appearance was at the Gateway Theatre, Chester, which was packed out. I seemed to be getting a lot of laughter in places I hadn't expected it. I found that the stage cat was giving a rival performance behind me, and that some of his antics might be construed as a cat's commentary on my best passages. The real value of these personal appearances came in the question period at the end of my remarks. I learned what staff were really concerned about. Things were brought to my notice which I would not otherwise have learned. In deciding to make these personal appearances I suppose that I was to some extent influenced by my own experiences of listening to General Montgomery (as he then was) talking to his troops before battle. This brought home to me the confidence which can be generated by the man at the top talking directly to large numbers of his men of all ranks instead of relying on written messages or second hand accounts of what had been said elsewhere.

Departmental information

Important though corporate information is, the more important priority is to ensure that there are agreed and effective systems for ensuring that information is filtering downwards about the policies and objectives of the council and those of the department. Many of the methods listed in Appendix 8.1 are as appropriate to departmental as to corporate information. However, the problem of informing staff cannot be solved by regular written information, however competently this is done. Some staff simply do not read departmental circulars; others do not digest them. There is no substitute for face to face communication. Introducing regular briefing sessions, on the lines adopted by many of the country's most successful industrialists, may sound simple. In practice it is not so and it may be wise to start with a pilot scheme and get help from a body like the Industrial Society which has done so much in this field not only for commerce and industry, but the public service as well.

The chief executive should recognize that the larger his organization, the greater the problem of adequate communication. He needs to ensure that all his departmental heads recognize that there is a problem. He must make everyone face up to it and agree some procedures, whether briefing sessions or otherwise, which are workable. The problem is at its most acute in departments which have many field workers or a large area organization. Staff who work away from the centre often feel neglected. Special care must be taken to ensure that outlying staff know what is going on and that systems are developed which cater for the field or case worker who only pays intermittent visits to his or her base.

Where there are important changes to well established procedures or working practices, the chief executive should set a good example by arranging teach-ins or other face to face learning sessions to supplement the necessary written revisions.

Councillors know-how

The day has long since gone when new councillors were put onto one minor committee and expected to keep their mouth shut for at least twelve months. All councillors expect a fair share of work and look to the administration to help them to perform their role successfully. Nearly all councils at the time of reorganization in 1974 felt obliged to introduce ways and means for the councillors to learn about the new authority, its functions and area. All councillors were to a degree new councillors in 1974 and there was a conscious effort throughout the length and breadth of the land to involve councillors fully in setting the new councils to work.

Many of the devices then introduced have been carried forward. One reason has been that with more 'clean sweep' elections, i.e. the whole council retiring together and in the case of counties after a four year term, changes in the composition of councils have been more radical.

Because this has been an area of recent attention and development, it may well be that little will need to be done to improve it. The following is a check list of some of the ways in which councillors can be informed of the procedures and policies of the authority.

1 Provision of members' library and information room possibly staffed by a librarian/research officer full- or part-time.

2 Information packs for new councillors comprising standing orders, budgets and general information about the area and functions of the authority, (and possibly a copy of the *Councillors Handbook* published by the Municipal Journal and written jointly by the author and Professor J. D. Stewart.)

3 Addresses and telephone numbers of councillors; office phone numbers of principal officers (perhaps home numbers too).

4 Information packs related to the work of particular committees for new members of the committees.

5 Seminars and teach-ins of a general character for all councillors for example, on the area and its characteristics, problems facing the authority or on procedural matters to help councillors to take more effective part in debates.

6 Seminars for committee members to inform them fully of past activity and policy and to consider the future. Such seminars may last for a whole day, or even be residential.

The chief executive should review what is being done and make it as comprehensive and effective as possible. The time taken to mount effective seminars should not be underestimated. There are nevertheless great benefits to be obtained in bringing councillors together with officials to discuss areas of concern, away from the routine agenda and business of a committee. With councillors spending time at party caucus meetings, as well as in committees, there is more need for the administration to ensure that new councillors know the facts and are not reliant upon morsels of information from the old guard.

Conclusion

The chief executive is in a unique position by personal example and endeavour to help to ensure that all staff in the council's employ are ready to puff out their chest and assert that their authority is as good as or better than any in the country. This must be the objective of the chief executive's conduct of internal relations.

NOT THE NINE O'CLOCK NEWS

Just before I retired, we decided to make a video film about the approach to the Budget. Retrenchment in public expenditure had just begun to bite and some explanation of policy changes seemed more than justified. The audio-visual staff at a teachers training college provided the studio and the equipment – unfortunately only in black and white. I and the public relations officer wrote an outline script. Felicity Goody, a BBC Manchester presenter, was hired to help generally and to conduct the interviews. She did a first class professional job. The whole thing was shot in two days and then edited down to 25 minutes. This was one of the weakest areas for the training college did not have the equipment to make possible a smooth and professional change from one 'scene' to the next. Some chairmen were invited to participate (though the film was seen really as management talking to staff) and some did not wish to follow the script or take directions from anyone. Felicity Goody was asked to assume responsibility for editing out the contributions which simply did not fit in or were too long or the like. When finished the film was shown to staff at about ten different locations. I went to all or nearly all the showings, to answer questions and invite discussion. I suppose the general verdict was 'Eight out of ten for trying'. I would not repeat the exercise unless colour was available and technical help to a higher standard than before for editing and final production. Our product was too amateurish to be regarded as wholly successful.

Appendix 8.1

CHECK LIST OF POSSIBLE CHANNELS OF COMMUNICATION

1 Staff magazine or newsletter; the effort involved in regular production is often underestimated.

2 Information enclosed with pay cheque. Used sparingly this can be effective, particularly for matters of personal importance to staff.

3 Leaflet or broadsheet handed to staff as they arrive at place of work. Distributed in this way there is sometimes a better chance of the information being read than if the material is sent to departments for circulation. This approach can be effective for major topics, e.g. the budget, adopting of some new policies or the like.

4 Short single-side information sheet placed over a period at places where staff congregate, for example staff canteens, sports clubs, as well as being made available in offices and elsewhere.

5 It will be normal to provide a copy of the council's annual report to each staff member. The possibility of writing some part of this for the benefit of staff should be kept in mind; staff are an important part of the general readership for any report prepared in accordance with section 4 of the Local Government Planning and Land Act 1980 and the guidance issued by the Department of the Environment.

6 With the greater availability at reasonable cost of video equipment, it may be possible for larger authorities to script and produce a short video film about some aspect of current policy, for example the budget, an early retirement scheme or the like. This can then be shown at advertised locations and enable a message to reach a wider audience than could readily be achieved by conventional means. Several companies use this technique to enable the managing director to speak to outlying staff once a year. So much that is written for staff remains unread. The video presentation fits moreover in with the changing habits of society everywhere.

GRASS ROOTS UPWARDS

A staff suggestion scheme provides a formal machinery for ideas about improving the organization to flow upwards. It should not of course be the only or even the principle means for staff to suggest ways of improving efficiency. One of its values is to provide a safety valve so that good ideas rejected by middle management can nevertheless be got forward for impartial assessment. Cheshire's scheme was largly a copy of IBM's (why reinvent the wheel). I believe in personally chairing the panel (including union representation) to ajudicate on suggestions. It always surprised me how many departments seemed unwilling to accept that changes in established methods could possibly be beneficial. I learned a lot from the reaction of managers to schemes submitted for their comments. Results from staff suggestion schemes are unlikely to be spectacular, but in considering communications, particularly in a large authority, they should not be overlooked.

9 Industrial relations

The chief executive must have a view about trade union matters. He must be prepared to take a lead in developing productive management/union relations at the local level.

It is not a role he can easily avoid, for it has been calculated that there are twice as many trade union members in the public service as in the private sector – probably about 80% as against 40%. Not only that, the public service unions have been markedly militant in recent years. The chief executive may have to deal with nothing more serious than modest industrial unrest, perhaps stemming from a feeling that incomes policies are applied by Government more rigorously against the public service than the private sector. He may on the other hand find himself in the centre of a strike which brings some part of the council's activities to a full stop with consequent disruption of some service to the public.

The chief executive should not be deterred from doing what he can at local level simply because so much is settled at the centre. Wages, salaries and conditions of service are largely settled in national negotiations conducted between the trade unions and the employers' representatives in one or other of the many national joint negotiating committees. If a strike is called or selective industrial action, it will usually be called by the headquarters of the union. The fact that there tends to be a great deal of centralization with little scope for 'plant bargaining' on lines common in industry, must not become an excuse for inactivity. There is much that can be done at local level to foster good industrial relations.

Local machinery

Nearly all authorities have established machinery for union consultation. This should be reviewed regularly to see that it fits today's working situation, and takes account of today's climate of opinion. It may have become too formal, or too centralized, or too cumbersome. On the other hand, what at one point in time could be dealt with over the telephone may at another require formal reference to an established committee. The object of the review is to keep the machinery in tune with the times and to have a comprehensive agreement covering negotiations, consultation, grievances and disciplinary matters. Trade union consultation on a wide range of matters is regarded as necessary and desirable. However, it does tend to slow down the already slow process of decision taking in local government. Consultation must therefore be seen as a means to an end and not as an end in itself.

The political angle

With party politics firmly embedded in reorganized local government, the chief executive will find himself under pressure to adopt a stance in relation to the unions and solutions to industrial relations problems which fit the doctrines of the majority party. It is no part of the chief executive's job to substitute his views for those of the majority party. It is, however, his duty to see that he thinks through the probable consequences of the preferred policy and sees that these are understood by the political leaders. Whilst some leaders have wide experience of trade union negotiations, disputes and so forth, others are ingenuous and need guidance. They do not appreciate the long term problems which may be created by the short term taking-up of postures or views.

Areas in which difficulties often arise include:

1 An authority may wish to make a statement of its opinion on an issue to be decided at national negotiating level, or indeed to reach a local decision in advance of a national settlement.

2 In the face of strike action, an authority may wish to encourage the crossing of picket lines; to promise rewards for non-strikers; punishments for strikers; or other action contrary to generally accepted trade union policies.

3 An authority may wish to pass resolutions in support of strikers, or take some more positive steps to support strikers or their families.

The chief executive may not be able to prevent the taking of steps which he believes to be unwise, but he should do all he can to ensure that they are not taken in the dark. He must accept that some councillors will not want a dispassionate assessment of the situation and that advice may be resented. That is no reason for the chief executive to throw his hand in; equally he must display sensitivity and show that he accepts that the decision is not his to make. By adopting a neutral stance to the unions, and by a fair and even-handed approach, the chief executive can play a crucial part in keeping industrial relations in his authority on an even keel.

TIME TO FIGHT ANOTHER DAY

At around 1978, the time when there was much trade union interest in the refuse collection service, the dustmen in Warrington came out on strike over a bonus dispute. The borough council urged house-holders to take their refuse to the county council refuse disposal tip. It was not far away, but served a much wider area than Warrington itself. The National Union of Public Employees instructed their members at the county council tip not to handle the privately deposited rubbish which was beginning to cause problems. The director of highways, my personnel officer and his industrial relations expert met me to discuss what should be done. We looked at the firm line. Probably the county council employees would have obeyed an instruction – or at least some of them – to move the private rubbish. Those who disobeyed (and it seemed likely there would be some) would have to be disciplined. NUPE might retaliate by asking their members in other council tips to take action in support. The union might also try and get dustmen in other towns who used the same tip to take sympathetic action. This would have been a pity as the Warrington dispute looked capable of early settlement. The difficulties at the county council tip were not insuperable in the short term. A strong line was taken on an attempt to lock the gate to the tip area and so prevent private householders from Warrington using it, but for the rest we decided to back away from any sort of con-frontation. We asked managers to swallow their irritation at not being able to manage the tip as they would have wished. The risks were greater than the benefits. In fact the Warrington dispute was settled in a week or so. There are occasions to stand and fight, but the decision to do so must be the result of a cool and dispassionate assessment of all the factors (which will include the personalities) involved.

Communication

Chapter 8 stresses the need for well thought out and regular com-munication to staff, so that the views of management are put across with conviction and so that reasons for policies and decisions are explained. Staff are rightly suspicious if the only communications they receive are sent out when trouble is brewing. If it is to be effective, communication needs to be continuous.

Special care needs to be taken with communications during the course of an industrial dispute. If there are agreements with the unions about communications during disputes they must be scrupulously followed. Nothing is more likely to exacerbate a dispute than a feeling that the employers have gone behind the backs of the unions in communicating with their membership.

Central scrutiny

If there is one part of personnel work which needs some degree of central control within the authority, it is industrial relations. A single trade union may have members in many different departments. It is all too easy for the union to divide and rule if each department is allowed to pursue its own ideas and reach its own agreement with the union. Important union issues must be dealt with if not by, at least in consultation with the centre. This is a vital part of the work of the personnel officer, who may if he is lucky have one member of his team who specializes in union matters. The role of the specialist adviser on industrial relations is as yet largely undeveloped in local government. In the larger authorities, especially in the more militant parts of the country, the number of these advisers is likely to increase over the next decade. The chief executive should only take a decision on industrial relations matters after seeking the advice which is available from the personnel officer and his staff. There is no area of decision-taking more full of pitfalls for the unwary than in the field of authority/union relations.

TO JOIN OR NOT TO JOIN

A problem which confronts the chief executive and chief officers is whether or not they can belong to one of the larger trade unions in local government. The National Association of Local Government Officers (NALGO) is likely to be seen as the obvious choice. I was a member of NALGO for many years and in Berkshire took a hand in organizing some of their social activities and appearing as a lecturer at the national residential course for committee clerks. Of course NALGO in those days was not in membership of the TUC nor had it adopted the militant attitudes prevalent today. When I was appointed Clerk of Cheshire County Council I resigned. I did not think it possible to be a member of the trade union with whom I would negotiate on behalf of the council. I felt that my credibility with councillors would be impaired and that my position would be ambivalent. Later on I felt reinforced in my judgement by the possibility that as a NALGO member I might be called upon to strike or negotiate some privileged exemption for myself. Not all my colleagues in other authorities shared my view at the time, and of course circumstances vary between one place and another. Fortunately the increasing strength and ability of trade unions for professionals and their Federation makes the issue of joining one of the large unions less important than it was.

Conclusion

Active and sometimes militant trade unionism has been part of the local government scene for over two decades. Trade unions, whilst protecting their members' interests can be helpful and cooperative and ensure that new procedures, organization and methods of working are brought in with minimum trouble. They can raise points which might otherwise be overlooked and secure fairer terms for staff. Trade unions can also be awkward and inflexible. They may use their industrial muscle to try and dictate to the local councillors what the authority's policy ought to be in a way that some councillors would regard as beyond the objects of the union and an unwarranted interference with local democracy. When trade unions act in these ways, the chief executive must not let his own or his council's irritation or exasperation cloud his or his council's judgement. Right is rarely confined to one side of the table.

To be able to fulfil the roles outlined, the chief executive needs to know the trade union leaders (both paid and unpaid) with whom he will have to deal. He should not only make contact when disputes are threatened, but set up occasional informal and friendly meetings when he and the personnel officer can talk with local and regional leaders without the pressure of having to solve some issue. He should try and make contact with national leaders or their representatives for example at conferences and get to know as much as he can about their private attitudes and thinking.

If the chief executive is known to the union leaders with whom his council must deal, he stands a better chance of playing a decisive role in both peaceful and disputatious times.

10 Intervention

When I am wrong, make me ready to change.
When I am right, make me easy to live with.

A chief executive has an interventionist role. To assert this is not to deny that more of his time will be spent in oiling the machinery, in removing causes of friction and unobtrusively checking that the engine is in a high state of tune.

But intervene he must from time to time when departmental action appears to be taking the authority on a wrong course. Intervention should not be a weekly or monthly affair. To be effective it must be infrequent, a reserve of power, effective because it is sparingly used. The need for constant intervention implies that some part of the machinery is in need of overhaul – someone somewhere is not performing. The cause of the trouble needs to be sought out and a remedy found. The chief executive cannot do other people's work for them.

Intervention must not be confused with interference. Some managers like to prove their virility and assert their status by constant interference in the work of others. A chief executive who breathes down the neck of his colleagues is as bad as one who shrinks from the action he knows to be needed. Somehow a balance must be struck between the two extremes of interference and non intervention.

It is not easy to categorize the areas in which intervention may be needed. Perhaps the most obvious is where a policy which a department or committee may wish to pursue will adversely affect the authority in areas outside the responsibility of the department or committee concerned. For example, the policy may cause problems with Government or with other local authorities or with trade unions.

The chief executive, where policy is concerned, should be able to provide a wider perspective. This will sometimes throw up problem areas which others more directly concerned have failed to observe.

COHERENT POLICY

The Conservatives on Cheshire County Council never willingly embraced comprehensive education. When it was still descretionary in the 1960s the Education Committee was digging itself in to defend the pattern of grammar and secondary modern schools established post-World War II. At the same time, the council had accepted that it would fully play its part in the development of Runcorn New Town and the town development schemes at Ellesmere Port and Winsford – designed to assist Liverpool's overspill problem. These three schemes involved substantial programmes of school building. It seemed obvious to me that the Labour Government would not provide capital allocations or loans for building grammar schools in these expanding areas. There was a clear dichotomy between the council's general policy and that of the Education Committee. The chairman of the council who shared my concern, arranged a discussion in his room with senior members of the Education Committee and the Director of Education (a lifelong opponent of the comprehensive theory). After much coming and going, the Education Committee agreed that in the expanding areas, the school building programme would accept without qualification the need for comprehensive schools. Intervention avoided what might have been a damaging dispute over educational policy in the New Town, Ellesmere Port and Winsford.

There is another area where the chief executive's ability to stand back from day-to-day matters may persuade him that intervention is needed. This is where the level of performance of a senior officer is seen to be inadequate but the officer is protected by the understandable loyalty and support of departmental colleagues. Many heads of departments are fiercely defensive of staff whose work standards have plummeted or who have been overpromoted or who for other reasons no longer measure up. It is never easy to solve problems of this sort. But accepting that there is a problem and that it must be faced is the first step to success. The chief executive may need to intervene to secure that this first step is taken.

Yet a third area for intervention may arise when a significant number of complaints are made about some part of the organization's work. Alternatively there may be recurring errors, causing embarrassment or worse. There may be delays in return of land charges or decisions on planning applications or notification of student grants. Creditors may complain of delays in payment on contract work. Concern may be expressed about the award of benefits, places in old peoples homes, allocation of home helps or housing repairs. The field is immense, and there will always be such areas of complaint or concern. It requires judgement to know when to intervene and when to take a more relaxed view, relying on departmental skill to do all that is necessary.

In truth, the whole area of operations of the authority must be open to the possibility of intervention. To select some for purposes of illustration does not mean that they will be the only or indeed the most usual in any one person's experience.

RESOLUTE NOT RUTHLESS

Following one of my visits to industrialists in Cheshire, this time Chester Barrie, I asked one of the directors who had returned from a spell working in the USA, what he had learned about suit-making there. 'Nothing', he replied, for British production methods were superior to American in many cases. 'You must have learned something' I continued. 'I guess' he replied 'I learned the need to be ruthless. That is something the Americans are much better at, when it's necessary'.

I never found it easy to take the action which my intelligence sometimes told me was necessary. But with experience I found that you could, so to speak, armourplate yourself, so that you did not avoid doing what you knew needed to be done. In most situations you can do a great deal to make things easier for those affected.

As clerk of the Magistrates Courts Committee I wanted to see all sessional divisions follow the boundaries of the reorganized local authorities. Over the years I achieved this, but it meant a fair amount of upheaval for staff. This was made as painless as possible by such measures as protecting rights to a parking place, or special hours of work, or by paying travel allowances, all agreed with the unions. To be resolute (which I prefer to 'ruthless') does not mean that you must be insensitive. But whatever word one uses, there is always a need to square up to the problem and be ready to take on board the consequences of action to solve it.

If it is difficult to lay down any guide lines as to *when* to intervene; it is relatively easier to erect a few sign posts as to *how* to do it, and how *not* to do it.

1 The timing of intervention is important. Nothing is more irritating and bad for working relations than the chief executive who has not bothered to read draft policy statements sent to him, but wants to put his oar in at the stage of final approval. The chief executive must find time personally to look at and appraise the policy drafts which come from departments. Some will be more important than others – for example the structure or local plan for the area prepared under the Town and Country Planning legislation. The chief executive should ideally provide his input at an early formative stage. However, in a busy authority, this is a counsel of perfection. Some drafts of policy statements will perforce land on the chief executive's desk without any prior involvement on his part. If he intends to intervene, he must do so as soon as he receives it, not just when the report is ready for final approval.

2 Intervention is best done on a face-to-face basis. It is unwise to write a long memorandum of dissent or apparently critical enquiry as the first step. Word of mouth statements can be varied quickly by later statements; the emphasis can be changed; false points can be abondoned. A document of written intervention can be copied and circulated and be used by the recipient as a rallying call to defend the threatened position. It may seem easier to send a written message because there is a degree of insulation from the result. But the chief executive is not like a bomber pilot whose mission is ended when the bombs are away. The chief executive has to get results. This means carrying others with him, convincing them of his point of view. He is unlikely to succeed by recording his view in a memorandum and hoping for the best. There will nevertheless be occasions when something has to be put in writing for the record and possibly for self-protection. Such a record should be made at the end of the debate and not at the beginning.

3 If the intervention is to secure a change in attitude or working practice, time must be allowed for the new idea to sink in. The status quo may be defended for no better reason than that it is understood. New ideas are rarely embraced on being first unveiled. The chief executive must be patient, and in his programme allow time for the rejection factor. It may take two or more attempts before the attempted transplant is successful. So the process must be started well before the change is needed. This is as true of councillors as it is of officers. 'Deferment for further consideration' does not necessarily imply hostility to a report presented to a committee. It is more likely to be an example of the need for time to adjust to the possibility of change.

ADJUSTING TO CHANGE

Electoral areas quickly get out of balance when there is the level of population growth experienced post-war in Cheshire. Because of this

I suggested to the committee concerned that a review of electoral divisions should be undertaken to cure these imbalances, some constituencies having three or four times the number of voters as compared with the average. The review was to come into force for the next county council election. My senior electoral registration officer worked hard and long (a little too long perhaps) and finally produced a very sound scheme which I needed to amend only in detail before presenting it to the committee shortly before the elections. It was approved without much discussion. At the council meeting it was a very different story. Every member whose constituency was affected by the revisions (or so it seemed) spoke up in violent opposition. I did my best to explain why fears were unjustified and why something needed to be done in fairness to the electorate. I experienced a hostility to me on the part of the council which I had never experienced before – or since, as I persevered in defence of the proposals. But I had to accept defeat and the report was rejected. In my room afterwards I kicked myself for not having put up an interim report, for not having got the final report forward at a greater distance from polling day – in short for skimping on the preparation of the ground, I simply had overlooked the rejection factor – always high where members' interests are involved. I was somewhat mollified when a few days later I was asked to rush forward proposals for a mini-review which would cure the worst cases but avoid some of the more contentious parts of the original proposals.

4 The intervenor should bear in mind throughout that he may be wrong. The detached stance referred to earlier is a source of strength. It may throw up for discussion a matter which those closer to the action have failed to observe. Distance can also make it difficult to see detail, and there is always the possibility that assimilation of the detail may alter the picture as it appeared at first. So the chief executive, whose judgement is that some matter requires his intervention, should enter on the task with humility. He may after all have got it wrong.

Intervention, needed and fully justified, may nevertheless be construed as interference. The action taken may be resented, however sensitively the opening moves are made. This is one reason for asserting that it should be an activity to be indulged in sparingly, with due caution.

There is one way in which this role of the chief executive can be made infinitely more acceptable to his colleagues. It arises if the chief executive is seen to be ready to intervene for and on behalf of his colleagues, to take their side and help them to press their case. If he is only seen as an adversary he is likely to have much less success than if he is seen as impartially striving to get the right results, ready to take on anyone when the occasion demands. There are many ways in which 'supportive' intervention of this sort can take place. A departmental matter may be supported by the chief executive, after consultation with the departmental head, by personal representation to a ministry, members of Parliament or others with power to influence the outcome. A chief officer's view may be vigorously supported by the chief executive before a committee or the full council. An officer threatened with disciplinary action may be assisted by the chief executive's efforts to ensure a fair and maybe merciful result.

If the chief executive is seen to care, to be prepared to take on all-comers, then his intervention in ways earlier described will be accepted by his colleagues as part of his duty to oversee the totality of the affairs of the authority.

MAKING USE OF CONSULTANTS

I made more use of consultants than some of my colleagues one of whom remarked disdainfully 'They bring to every problem a fresh breath of ignorance'. Consultants are seen to be independent. I doubt if staff would have talked so freely to an in-house researcher as to the charming lady consultant of the Industrial Society who undertook two studies of departmental communications. The recommendations of consultant firms may also have greater credibility with councillors and the public. Sometimes credibility is crucial, as for example the study of the costs of local government reorganization carried out by P A Management Consultants. Cheshire's own assessment would have been considered suspect.

The use of consultants is a useful tool for the interventionist. With proper briefing, a consensus about conclusions, and commitment to implementation of recommendations, the cost of consultants can be more than justified.

11 Public relations and the world outside

The chief executive should be the public relations officer for his authority. That is, he should recognize that one of his prime tasks is to foster good and purposeful relations with the world outside, as well as to be responsible for relationships within the organization, dealt with in Chapter 8.

Some chief executives see public relations mainly as the hiring of professional consultants to produce a range of glossy booklets or to take space in the London Underground between the underwear advertisements to extol the virtues of their district. Publications and advertising have a part to play but they are a means to an end and not an end in themselves.

Some chief executives appoint a public relations officer and then forget about him. If the PR officer is to succeed, he must report directly to the chief executive and have easy access to him at all times. A knowledge of the press, its ways of working, its attitudes and conventions is important, and the best PR officers have normally had experience somewhere in their career as reporters. Yet without the thrust which the chief executive uniquely can give, technical experience and ability will not be enough.

Some chief executives are scornful of public relations. They regard it as mere image building, and rightly point out that if the image does not match the reality, the effort will be wasted. This attitude overlooks the fact that the projection of an image can help to mould attitudes, to alter reactions and to promote change. Image building should be seen as part of the process of change, not as a substitute for it. Good public relations can help to improve performance and should not be regarded as a trendy gimmick.

Some chief executives fight shy of an active part in public relations because they think that it means taking on the 'front man' role, and they may prefer to stay in the background. Some chief executives

have in the past certainly made a contribution by successfully playing
the front man. The growth in party politics, however, will increase the
likelihood of a less prominent contribution. A powerful political
leadership anxious to hold the centre of the stage (and be seen to do
so) may require that the chief executive maintains a low profile. So
far as the media are concerned, he may have to adopt a civil service
stance, working largely in the background, unidentified, but
nevertheless guiding and assisting his political masters. However, this
will not always be the case. An even division of political power, a lack
of equilibrium, the absence of confident spokesmen may make
councillors unwilling to accept the parts which they might normally
be expected to play. Here the chief executive must try and be
positive, even if his personal inclination (or perception of his own
abilities) might dictate a lower-key role.

Whatever the personal role of the chief executive – and it will vary
in different political and economic situations – he should never let
public relations slip in his priority list. It is the activity of ensuring that
the authority's policies, objectives, problems and achievements are
known and explained to all those concerned. This means, in effect,
explaining them not only to the community at large but also to the
several bodies whose functions interface closely with those of the
authority, as well as to the special interest groups in the area. It is by
its nature a continuous process which can never be completed.

Even in a small authority, the web of relationships will be large and
it is impossible that all parts can receive the continuous personal
attention of the chief executive. Nevertheless he needs to be conscious of the size of web and have a view (which may change from
time to time) of the relative importance of the component parts.

Press and Media

By one means or another – press conferences, press lunches,
meeting editors individually or in groups – the chief executive needs
to get to know the local press, local radio and television reporters.
Most of the irritation felt by local government over its treatment in the
media stems from a failure of understanidng, in turn caused by a
failure to meet and talk. Papers and other media cannot live on a diet
of 'No comment'. The chief executive because of his position is often
able to say something which lesser officials would fight shy of. He is
often therefore the man whom reporters most wish to speak to.
Being accessible is part of good relations with the media. Being
accessible does not mean taking every telephone call personally or
responding to every invitation to comment. It is often a mistake to
speak off the cuff; but if a promise is made that a call will be returned,

the promise should be kept even if reflection on the inquiry leads to the conclusion that 'no comment' must be the response. The chief executive may be able to make use of the new conventions much used by Government spokesmen. These are (a) the 'non-attributable' statements, i.e. something which can be used but must not be attributed to anyone in particular – 'a spokesman said'; and (b) the 'non-quotable' statement. The latter gives confidential background information which cannot be used at the time it is given, but allows an informed report to be prepared but only published when the confidential embargo is removed. It is mainly useful where something sufficiently newsworthy is occurring, that a series of informal press briefings take place over a period (e.g. a long running industrial dispute). On the whole, both non-attributable and non-quotable statements are more likely to be used by the public relations officer than the chief executive, but they are devices worth bearing in mind.

There are times when the media are savagely critical, inaccurate or tendentious, and in recent years it has become more fashionable to criticize than to praise local government. Failures of impartiality, fairness and balance will occur. They are part of the public relations scene. They should not go unanswered or uncorrected, for example a letter of rebuttal may be prepared for the Leader or a Chairman to sign. Their existence, nevertheless, should not deflect the chief executive from a general willingness to be accessible, to inform, to explain and to answer questions. If a personal attack is made, it is not easy to maintain an open-handed posture, but in the long term the effort will be repaid.

Radio and television

Particularly where local radio covers the area of an authority, the chief executive will have opportunities to be interviewed or to take part in programmes. The same holds true of regional television. When these opportunities occur, they should be siezed. Very often the invitiations are personal. The radio or television producer may not just be looking for 'a spokesman' and will therefore not be happy with a substitute. The time factor is also important. Radio and television usually want the interview 'today' so that acceptance may involve personal inconvenience or rearrangement of the office or home diary. These sacrifices are worth making, because the audiences are so large and the potential impact so considerable. It is desirable that there is an understanding with the political leadership about radio and television appearances because the time factor will usually make it difficult to follow through a procedure for obtaining individual approval. If the opportunity is passed over, not only will it not recur; future invitations may not be forthcoming. By the same token, it is very desirable that the chief executive should be able to signal approval to chief and senior officers who may be uncertain whether or not to accept an invitation from radio or television.

As this chapter is concerned with principles and attitudes it is not the place to write in detail about techniques. There are courses of instruction in radio and television appearance and it is very worthwhile to take advantage of these, preferably on an 'in-house' basis so that a number of councillors and officers can all take advantage of instruction and practice.

Radio and television present a great challenge. Politicians and officials who are used to making long and patient statements, have the unusual discipline of trying to distil the essence of their position into a few minutes at most. The live appearance, whilst more stressful, prevents the editing which sometimes alters the sense of a recorded interview. But a recorded interview is a good way to start, for mistakes due to nerves can be corrected. Ideally the first live appearance should be as part of a panel, where the tensions are less.

Experience is a great help and there is truth in the axiom that the only way to learn is by doing it. However, no amount of skill in presentation will compensate for lack of knowledge of the subject matter. Better decline an invitation than appear and be asked questions on a subject about which one is inadequately briefed.

Every local authority should have thought-out and agreed procedures by which it can respond instantly to any request and can put forward for interview a chairman of a committee, councillor or senior official, with training, and preferably experience, in the medium concerned. Any chief executive who has not got such procedures of response has left a large part of his public relations work undone.

GOD'S GIFT TO COMMUNICATION

I recall one afternoon being called to the telephone from a meeting in London to see if I could possibly get to Manchester by 6 pm to appear on BBC's Look North programme following the news. The council had just sent out to every household in the county a leaflet explaining the proposals of the Royal Commission on Local Government Reorganization, which involved the destruction of the County of Cheshire. The BBC wanted to take a critical view of the expenditure involved in our information exercise: but they wished me to be there to respond. My wife and I were due to dine with the High Sheriff that evening near Chester, the dress for me being dinner jacket. A county car was dispatched to meet me at Manchester having collected my evening kit from home. Stuart Hall, the Look

North presenter kindly lent me his dressing room after the programme
to change. The interview itself was a 'hard-line' one i.e. one in which
the questioner is aggressive and tries to force the spokesman onto the
defensive. I was glad to have the chance to put Cheshire's views on a
programme watched by so many people. These included our host
who was quite surprised when I arrived later properly dressed and on
time. A colleague once remarked that I regarded TV as God's gift to
communication. 'He'll drop anything to go on the box' he added. I
suppose this story proves that he was right.

Special interest groups

Press, radio and television are the prinicpal means by which the local
authority can get its case across to the community at large. However,
within the community there are groups who may justify special
consideration. Circumstances will vary considerably between one
area and another. In some rural and residential areas, for example,
industry and commerce may be little represented. In others, there may
be few civic, amenity or ratepayers groups. This section is accordingly
something of a check list, not every part of which will apply to every
authority. The chief executive should periodically survey what his
authority are doing under the various headings. 'Keep your
friendships in good repair', said Dr Johnston – good advice for the
chief executive who wants the outside world to understand what his
authority are trying to achieve.

Industry and commerce

Industry and commerce nationally meet nearly 40% of the rate bill. In
some heavily industrialized areas the percentage may be higher. Yet
industry and commerce have no direct representation on the council,
and cast no votes at elections. If one adds in for good measure that the
town planning policies of many councils, backed by Government
policies on industrial development certificates, seemed designed to
ensure that industry was 'cribbed cabined and confined', it is not
difficult to understand that industry has felt unloved, and is now one of
the more vocal critics of rate levels and of local government. This
general picture is redeemed by the considerable number of authorities
who attempt to foster good relations with industry and commerce,
mainly those with a desire to increase the size or variety of the
employment base for their area.

   What can be done to ensure a better understanding between the
authority and its commercial and industrial interests? The following
suggestions may be worth exploring:

1 Consider arranging meetings with representatives of commerce and industry which go beyond the statutory requirement in section 13 of the Rates Act 1984, (which imposes a duty to consult in each financial year and before total estimated expenditure is determined). In some areas the regional office of the Confederation of British Industry has taken a lead in asking for meetings of this sort and has followed up with requests to examine particular areas of council activity to see if value for money is being obtained. It is unwise to start meetings which go beyond the statutory requirements if the council is antagonistic to commerce and industry because a dialogue which is started but then artificially confined, or even broken off, is probably worse than no dialogue at all.

If discussions can be continued over a period of years, industry will acquire a much better understanding of the constraints facing councils, the relatively small room for manoeuvre and the reasons for expenditure levels. They may even be persuaded that the local authority is run in an efficient way. On their side, the council's representatives may be alerted to areas of expenditure which to an outsider seem unjustifiable, and should acquire a better understanding of the problems faced by commerce and industry in their area.

If some general effort is made to explain the council's policies to the employers side of industry and commerce consideration should also be given to the regional organization of the TUC, so that parallel arrangements can be offered to those proposed for the employers' representatives.

2 Besides such general contacts, arranged through the CBI and local Chambers of Commerce, there is much to be gained by the chief executive arranging to visit the larger employers in his area. Something more than a pleasant lunch with the managing director should be aimed at. The chief executive should seek to leave the plant knowing at least:

a   the composition of the work force – white collar, blue collar; areas of recruitment, etc.;
b   main products;
c   means of transport of goods and employees to and from the plant;
d   any environmental or pollution problems;
e   possible plans for extension or contraction;
f   any special problems, particularly those where the local authority might be of help.

If such purposeful visits can be arranged, the chief executive being accompanied by some chief officers, useful links can be forged which can benefit both sides. For example, a large firm may undertake training activities which could be used by the local authority's personnel or vice versa. Or it may be possible to arrange short secondments on an interchange basis. Above all, both sides will get to know each other in a way which should be helpful for the future.

3 There may be scope in some councils for the cooption of a member or members to represent the interests of industry and commerce on committees where such representation is desirable. The constitution of some education committees provides for the cooption of a person with special knowledge of industry, but the persons appointed are sometimes better known for their political affiliations than their knowledge of the needs of industry. Many councils are averse to cooption in principle; and there is the problem of finding members who would be genuinely representative of the commercial or industrial interests they were expected to safeguard. In spite of these obstacles, the possibility of cooption should not be overlooked. With councils becoming increasingly party political, there is a danger of membership becoming the province of the politically active, the retired, and the housewife. The cooption to some committees of a knowledgeable businessman or woman would be no bad thing, but in the current climate of opinion the difficulties are sizeable.

Civic, ratepayers and amenity groups

The importance and standing of civic societies, ratepayers' associations and other pressure groups varies considerably from one area to another. In some areas they have considerable persuasive power with the local authority and may even field their own candidates at elections. In others, they contribute little, and their views are tolerated rather than sought and respected.

The chief executive should review periodically the relationship with these bodies so that they are used effectively for two-way communication between the authority and those with a special interest in the authority's work or some special part of it. Most of what has been said about industry and commerce is also relevant to these civic groups. They may justify the arrangement of regular meetings to explain the budget or policies of the authority. Their annual general meetings may provide a platform for the chief executive, by invitation, to speak about the work of his authority – a courtesy visit similar to that advocated in the case of major local firms. And some, particularly those concerned with civic amenities, will justify consultation on issues coming before the council, for example conservation and development issues coming before the town planning committee.

The other public authorities

Local authorities are not the only bodies whose activities impact upon the local community. There are the health authorities. There are the statutory undertakers providing gas, electricity, water and sewage services. There are others such as road and rail transport undertakings, docks, airfield operators, and the Post Office.

Sometimes the operational areas of these bodies are co-terminous with the boundaries of local authorities. More often they are not. Because information is not readily available for their own operational areas it is surprising how often these authorities will work in relative isolation from the local councils whose populations they serve. They may have their own estimate of likely population growth; their own perception as to what may happen to industry and commerce; their own ideas as to development of housing. The abolition of the Greater London Council and the Metropolitan County Councils must increase this type of difficulty in the largest urban areas in the country. Local authorities with their range of public services are the right bodies to improve and develop the interface between themselves and the other providers of services. One chief executive may not be able to take an effective initiative on his own. It may require a coordinated effort by a group of districts, or by a county and its districts for a better flow of information – in both directions – to be achieved. The chief executive and the chief planning officer should work closely together in this facet of the public relations of the authority. They should take the opportunities provided by the need to prepare or revise statutory plans required under town planning legislation, to arrange meetings at which top level representatives of other public bodies can join in a dialogue designed to shape the future on a better basis of knowledge and shared information. If the chief executive makes it known that he will personally attend such meetings, there is every chance that the other bodies will be represented at policy making level as well as competent technical level.

The chief executive should also make an effort to know his opposite number in these other public bodies. Much good can come from informal contacts. They can help to prevent an isolationist approach, as though local authorities were the only bodies concerned to provide public services in their area.

Civil service

Local government has been described as a partnership with central government. It goes without saying that the chief executive should know the prinicipal regional officers of the civil service in his area. He should also recognize that within the principal Departments there are views and perceptions about his authority built up over the years. Where the Department concerned has an inspectorial role, the view will be fairly continuous and less fragmentary, and therefore more likely to be up to date and accurate than one in a Department without inspectors. Departmental views and perceptions can be very helpful to a chief executive who wishes to be alerted to areas where efficiency levels or value for money are less than might be expected. There are but few authorities who do everything well. Past policies, past enthusiasms, past indifference, and past economies, all affect the standards achieved by a particular council. A wise chief executive will be anxious to learn where his authority is regarded as being a good performer and where performance could be improved. The impartial outside view of a Government Department can be most helpful to a chief executive. He need not – indeed should not – accept everything he is told as incapable of being challenged. Nevertheless, views from senior civil servants can help to pinpoint areas of weakness and so enable the chief executive to concentrate his efforts upon them.

AN OUTSIDE VIEW

Shortly after I took up my appointment, I arranged to see the Permanent or Deputy Secretary of the main Government Departments concerned with local government. I wanted to know how their departments saw the Chershire County Council. What were we doing well, what badly. Were there any long outstanding points of friction between us. Did they wish to enlist my support for any particular purpose. I found that these contacts were very helpful and informative. They also led to other contacts of value. I was introduced for example to the senior regional adviser for education in North West England and to the Ministry of Education's chief architect. I established a good working relationship with the divisional road engineer of the Ministry of Transport. In spite of recent difficulties I am sure that the concept of partnership between central and local government is the right one. Personal contact between officials on both sides can only help the concept to flourish.

Successful public relations

The following are a few suggestions which may help the chief executive in his approach to public relations:

1 However great the financial stringency, the chief executive should fight for some budget for public relations. The greater the problems facing the authority, the greater the need for the authority to explain its problems and what it is doing about them. It is an irony of life therefore that the public relations budget is often an early casualty of an economy drive.

2 When money is short, it is easy for public relations to grind down to the level of the commonplace – press releases, routine press conferences and answering enquiries. The chief executive needs to prize his staff from giving their whole attention to such commonplace activities in order to undertake some new work, project or enterprise.

3 The chief executive should see to it that the existence of a professional PR officer and staff does not hinder direct contact between the media and the chief and senior officers of the council. These are the people who know the answers. Good public relations officers ensure that the media find the right person and talk direct to him.

4 The biggest enemy of good communication is that patterns and stereotypes emerge. What was fresh and exciting when introduced becomes tired and stale with repetition. Today's piece of innovation is tomorrow's piece of boredom. The chief executive should take an interest in the routine communications emanating from his authority. His interest may well awaken some new ideas and produce some innovation.

5 There is very occasionally a time to say nothing, to be unavailable. There are battles which cannot be won, times when the media will be critical whatever is said by way of explanation or justification. To eleborate will merely provide more food for hostile comment. It is not easy to recognize these situations, but once recognized, a policy of 'No comment' may prevent further damage.

KNOWING WHEN TO CHANGE

When Cheshire had a very large building programme spread over a wide geographical area, it was hard to keep all councillors informed as to what was going on. We decided that it would be worth issuing with the council reports a pull-out picture supplement to illustrate the achievements of the council in the past six or eight weeks. This featured new buildings brought into service, activities of departments which lent themselves to pictorial illustration, staff who had achieved distinction and so forth. It was very well received, indeed I sometimes felt that for some councillors it was the only part of the papers which they bothered to look at.

After three years or so, the picture supplement looked stereotyped. We seemed to have said in pictures all we could say. So the supplement was stopped: no one mourned its passing.

12 Managing yourself

The chief executive is the highest paid officer within his authority. It is vital that he uses his time effectively and carefully. He should personally seek to give good value for money to his council. His example will set the tone for the whole administration. If the chief executive is never at his desk, never available, his senior colleagues will take their cue from him.

There are many temptations within the authority. The temptation to set up too many working parties – and what may be worse, to attend their meetings in person. The temptation to go to most meetings of most committees, instead of striking a balance along the lines suggested in Chapter 3. The temptation to accept every hospitable invitation extended by the mayor or chairman.

There are temptations which come from outside. The invitation to serve on a committee of a professional institute or society. The invitation to become an adviser to one of the associations of local authorities. The invitation to become a member of a governmental committee or working party – be it a Department of State, the National Economic Development Office, the British Standards Authority or one of that great proliferation of bodies undertaking research.

There are conferences which the chief executive can attend, many of them admirable in purpose. There are seminars and study days on subjects of topical interest and importance. There are requests to speak, to lecture, to give prizes at schools.

All these and many more will seek to distract the chief executive from the imperative need to be at his desk for a reasonable part of each working week.

All this may seem obvious. Yet most of those who deal regularly with local authorities will agree with the indictment that too rarely is the local authority officer – even at middle grade level – behind his desk and able to take any incoming telephone calls. He is more likely to be at a meeting or 'in conference'. If one adds in the restrictions on accessibility inherent in flexible working hours, there is certainly a case to answer.

The whole ethos of local authority work has until recent years militated against any consciousness of personal cost-effectiveness. Many people come into local government in the belief that it will allow them to seek professional perfection in a way that would be impossible if they practised their profession in the world outside. Others believe that service to the public cannot be expressed in pounds and pence.

If the chief executive were a partner in a firm providing services to clients, e.g. a solicitor or accountant, he would be required to bill his time against the clients concerned. This salutary discipline ensures that the partner does not undertake research or other work which the client cannot reasonably be asked to pay for at the end of the day. If work is undertaken the cost of which cannot be reimbursed, it will be undertaken knowingly and for good reason for example, to earn goodwill or because the research will be of permanent value. Few local authority officers are subjected to such a discipline, and except in a few cases it seems unlikely that the costs involved in setting up and operating such a system would be justified by any savings which might be achieved. What is needed is that every chief executive – and for that matter every senior officer – should by one means or another acquire a built-in feeling that his time is important and expensive to his authority.

An excellent starting point in acquiring this built-in feeling is to acquire knowledge as to how time is actually spent. Many writers on management have advocated this. Keeping a record, even a rudimentary one, will dispel many illusions. Anything less than three months is unlikely to lay a real foundation. It may be an interesting management exercise, but will not be long enough to create the built-in feeling that time is important and expensive and must only be given to subjects which are worthwhile. Worthwhile, that is, from the point of view of the employer who foots the bill, and for self-development, because in the long run that is good for the employer too.

KEEPING TRACK OF TIME

I kept a diary of my time for four months or more. My relentless secretary would appear each morning with the special diary in her hand and adjure me to bring it up to date. Because I know that I would find it a tiresome, if rewarding, exercise I divided each day into four parts. A simple record over a longer period seemed preferable to a detailed one, say every hour, for one or two weeks.

To my various 'clients' I gave code letters. The Personnel Committee A: the Policy Committee B, the Regional Economic Planning

Council C: County Council meeting D and so forth with a dustbin number say X for anything not specifically allocated.

Because I wanted to know what sort of work I did as well as for whom I did it. I gave code numbers to various recurring types of activity Original drafting, research, or 'thinking' 01: attendance at formally summoned meeting 02: giving a talk or paper 03: interviewing for selection of staff 04: informal discussion 05 and so forth. Inevitably a fair amount of time is spent in correspondence, discussion with your secretary, telephoning and other routine activities, and a special code for this was needed.

The codes in the diary can be transferred manually to a simple matrix each week, the horizontal columns providing the 'clients' and the vertical the types of work. In my case the data processing manager organized a simple programme to give me a monthly analysis. The four months analysis showed that I spent relatively little time (about 12%) 'thinking'. Outside activities accounted for nearly 25% of my time, and would have accounted for more if much of the travelling involved had not been done in my own time i.e. outside the four periods in the diary. (One conclusion was that this figure was too high). My main 'client' was the Local Government Reorganization Subcommittee for this was the time when Cheshire was fighting for survival. Activities under the aegis of the Personnel Committee came next – appointing staff, taking part in training, trade union matters and so forth.

The final analysis was interesting, but the real benefit was to make me conscious of my time and of the need to organize it better.

In particular, the chief executive needs to assess carefully the extent to which he can become involved in things that are 'good for local government'. Someone must advise the associations of local authorities. Someone must put the local government point of view to Government departmental committees. Someone must help to run the professional institutes and societies who contribute greatly to the efficiency of local authorities and their departments. Yet the chief executive who is asked to play a part should not automatically accept every invitation that comes his way. His council may be pleased at the mark of confidence in his ability which such an invitation implies. The council may believe, and rightly, that what he learns at the centre of things will be good for them. The trouble is that work is found for willing hands. The chief executive can become submerged in these extra-mural activities. He becomes incapable, because of lack of time, to give to his authority the leadership he should provide.

By travelling in his own time and by reading in the evenings and at weekends, the chief executive can, at some cost to his family life, take on more. In general terms, however, he should try and spend four working days out of five on matters which directly concern his own authority. A ration of one day per week on the business of other people than his employer is a good working guide. Of course there will be exceptions when with council approval greater demands can reasonably be accepted for short periods, for example to chair a Government committee of inquiry, to assume the presidency of a society, or to serve as a member of a board or commission for a limited term.

For those unwilling or unable to undertake an exercise in time-keeping on the lines advocated in this chapter, it is sobering to work out the basic daily rate of pay, and use this as a means of inculcating the feeling that time is important – and expensive. Some telephones are now equipped with monitors which display the minute by minute cost of any outgoing call. It would focus the mind even more if the machine were able also to clock up the salary figure.

UNREWARDING ACTIVITY

There are some matters where councillors will take their own decisions, and where the chief executive's influence can only be marginal. The choice of chairman of a committee, who should serve on which outside body, attend a conference and the like, will be determined by political and personal ambitions of councillors and pressures within the party machine. The chief excecutive should be wary of intervening in these areas. He need not shrink from giving his opinion if asked, or putting forward a view: but he should not be dismayed if his hopes or expectations are not realized. I learned this from experience when Sir Wesley Emberton, the chairman of the council, died suddenly. It was clear that the vice-chairman would succeed him, the real question being who would be the new vice-chairman. I busied myself on this issue, talking with senior councillors and as a result doing what I could to promote the cause of one candidate who seemed to command a large measure of support. However, when it came to the day, a councillor was elected vice-chairman whose name had never been broached by anyone. He made an excellent vice-chairman. I could have spent my time more profitably.

The secretary and the diary

The person who can best help the chief executive to maximize his performance in terms of time, is his secretary. These underpaid and sometimes underused helpmates to senior officers have a crucial role to play in seeing that the boss directs his attention to the right things at the right time. But the secretary cannot do this on her own. She and the chief executive must sit down together and work out an approach to the problem of the diary. If some guide lines can be agreed, there will be better use of the chief executive's time and less wasted effort.

The experienced secretary knows that the meeting which the chief executive forecasts to last one hour will certainly take one and a half. He is an optimist, she is a realist. She will not programme anything else for two hours to be on the safeside.

The chief executive thinks that he is indestructible. The experienced secretary knows that the chief executive is below par on the day after a strenuous series of meetings in London. She will draw a line through the morning after, so that time can be found to catch up.

The chief executive thinks that he is indispensable. The experienced secretary knows that many activities go equally well without him. She will ascertain the availability of someone to deputize and so make it easier for the chief executive to be selective. Self denial does not come easily to most chief executives. The experienced secretary will help him not to go everywhere and take on everything.

The experienced secretary knows that the chief executive tends to put off doing the creative things which make greater demands than the routine ones. She will quietly and insistently remind him of the things he has left undone. The notes for a speech to the Chamber of Commerce; the vetting and approval of a new manpower plan; a discussion paper for a committee or a society – all the difficult things which are stuck in the pending tray. The chief executive should never resent timely reminders of matters of this sort. The experienced secretary will not mind if he does, and will not be deflected.

The experienced secretary knows that her chief executive loses all sense of time when locked in discussion in his room. It may be a visiting dignitary, a councillor, a colleague from a neighbouring authority or a member of the council's staff. If he is the sort of chief executive from whom such discussions degenerate into an escapism from work, the experienced secretary will try and break the trance. A telephone call awaits urgent return; a colleague needs ten minutes before the end of the day; or the post room shuts in fifteen minutes – by these and other discreet announcements the chief executive can be reminded that his time must not be squandered. Of course, there are vital discussions to which no time limits should be set; but the experienced secretary knows that there are not many of these.

The chief executive must learn to manage himself and his time. If he cannot manage himself he is unlikely to be able to manage others.

He may be a great solo performer, but the chief executive's job demands more than a virtuoso performance. There have been a few notable exceptions to this principle, but in general it is true. The chief executive needs to know himself. If he works best in the morning, he should keep some mornings free for thinking and writing, selecting routine items for the afternoon.

The chief executive needs to take good care of himself if he is to take care of others. The amount of driving he does, the amount of travelling, the amount of drinking, the number of speeches, the inroads into his holiday or weekend time, all need watching. The experienced secretary can be a great help in making the chief executive pay attention to what he does with his time. Indirectly this will help him to know more about himself. A proper partnership between chief executive and secretary will not produce perfection. But the results will be infinitely superior to those obtained by chief executives who use their secretaries only to take dictation and make all their appointments personally in a pocket diary, because they do not trust anyone else to get it right.

FINALE

With my vast store of wisdom it seems a pity not to use it all. But thou O Lord knowest that I want to have a few friends at the end. Restrain me from speaking on every topic on all occasions. Give me wings to get to the point of a matter. Help me to avoid putting everything right. And above all keep me from immersion in tiresome details.

Anon.

Index